MW01113807

Empower Yourself for an Amazing Career

National Association of Book Entrepreneurs (NABE)
Pinnacle Book Achievement Award Winner
Summer 2012

Empower Yourself for an Amazing Career

Blanca De La Rosa

Foreword by: José Antonio Tijerino
25% of Proceeds to be donated to the
Hispanic Heritage Foundation

BALBOA
PRESS

A DIVISION OF HAY HOUSE

Balboa Press books may be ordered through booksellers or by contacting:

Balboa Press
A Division of Hay House
1663 Liberty Drive
Bloomington, IN 47403
www.balboapress.com
1-(877) 407-4847

Because of the dynamic nature of the Internet, any web addresses or
links contained in this book may have changed since publication and
may no longer be valid. The views expressed in this work are solely those
of the author and do not necessarily reflect the views of the publisher,
and the publisher hereby disclaims any responsibility for them.

The author of this book does not dispense medical advice or prescribe the use
of any technique as a form of treatment for physical, emotional, or medical
problems without the advice of a physician, either directly or indirectly. The
intent of the author is only to offer information of a general nature to help
you in your quest for emotional and spiritual well-being. In the event you use
any of the information in this book for yourself, which is your constitutional
right, the author and the publisher assume no responsibility for your actions.

Any people depicted in stock imagery provided by Thinkstock are models,
and such images are being used for illustrative purposes only.

Certain stock imagery © Thinkstock.

Print information available on the last page.

ISBN: 978-1-4525-3758-0 (e)
ISBN: 978-1-4525-3757-3 (sc)
ISBN: 978-1-4525-3797-9 (hc)

Library of Congress Control Number: 2011914436

Balboa Press rev. date: 12/18/2018

Praises for Blanca De La Rosa and Empower Yourself
for an Amazing Career

"Useful, inspirational, and Practical guide
for empowering women"

"Finding your way on the career path is often a difficult journey. Author Blanca De La Rosa offers a lantern; drawing on her experiences gleaned from thirty years at a large corporation . . . the author candidly admits her faults and missteps."—*New York Book Festival 2012—Honorable Mention*

"This valuable book of insights can be used by anyone, in any job, at any level, who is striving to get ahead. De La Rosa is honest, revealing her career missteps and faults. She learned along the way to look at her career in a different way, and that ability and her keen insight brought a level of satisfaction that no job title can convey."—*New England Book Festival 2012*

"An executive outlines best practices for climbing the corporate ladder. An accessible guide for empowering women to advance in their careers."—*Kirkus Reviews*

"I love your book. I started it one evening and didn't put it down until I was done. Saying "great job" is an understatement. I am so impressed with your tenacity and focus. The peacock is a brilliant symbol."—*Kay Zinngrabe, Project Manager*

"I finished your book over the weekend! Congratulations on a wonderful accomplishment! It was actually the perfect time for me to read something like that—very inspirational and made me realize some things about my own career and personal life."—*Alex Pascarella, Strategic Pricing Advisor*

". . . he leído lo suficiente para apreciar cuán inspiradora es tu historia, Blanca, no sólo para mi hija, sino para todos los latinos . . . . un ejemplo que tenemos que perseguir nuestros sueños!—*Rodrigo E. Diaz, Manager Business Planning & Analysis*

"Strongly agree with many of the points that you made; particularly the over-arching theme of attitude (and others perception of yours) playing a pivotal role in how a career develops.—*Christian Petterson, Refinery Coordinator*

"Ms. De La Rosa's experience and her remarkable and continuing journey in the corporate world provide an "insider's" guide for successfully coping with and meeting the challenges that confront most of us . . . . It is very readable, well-presented . . . Useful Inspirational and Practical Guide."—*Paul Premo, Energy Economist Consultant*

De La Rosa provides excellent, practical, career development advice for young professionals . . . . outlining strategies, insights, and self-reflection on what may have slowed her career progression. The book is easy to read and at times inspirational . . . . I recommend this book to anyone desirous of achieving their ultimate potential in a corporate environment."—*Steve Traylor, Petroleum Products Trader*

CONTENTS

Pride of the Peacock xi

Foreword xiii

Introduction xvii

Chapter 1: Your Career—A Journey, not a Destination 1

Chapter 2: The Corporate Culture—Is it for You?.............. 7

Chapter 3: Managing a Bad Manager 13
            A Rocky Start to My Corporate Career................22

Chapter 4: A Holistic Approach to Your Career................ 31
            i.   Go Above and Beyond 35
            ii.   Commit to Continuous Learning....................39
            iii. Master Your Current Assignment 43
            iv.   Differentiate Yourself from the Competition 47
            v.   Improve Your Communication Skills 51
            vi.   Establish Yourself as a Leader...........................57
            vii. Get off the Fence 61
            viii. Find a Mentor...65
            ix.   Networking 69
            x.   Project Confidence 73

Chapter 5:   Career Failure 77
             My Career Hits a Roadblock 82

Chapter 6:   Managing Change Effectively 96

Chapter 7:   Female Leaders—Balancing Power Issues 102

Chapter 8:   Are Women Their Own Worst Enemies? 109

Chapter 9:   Balancing Career and Family 117

Chapter 10: The Glamorous World of Business Travel 123

Chapter 11: Developing the Road Map of your Career 131

Chapter 12: Assessing the Journey of Your Career 138

PRIDE OF THE PEACOCK

Peacocks are deeply symbolic birds. However, the exact symbolism and significance of their feathers often depends on the culture and the context in which they appear.

Peacock feathers represent pride, nobility, and glory.

Peacocks eat poisonous plants with no adverse effects, making them a symbol of incorruptibility, immortality, and the ability to thrive in the face of suffering.

Peacocks have been associated with openness, since they proudly display everything when they spread their tails.

Peacocks can at times be regarded as vain and foolish birds and their presence a symbol of indulgent decadence. In his regard, their feathers represent a sign of vanity, as well as excessive pride, especially in personal appearance.

FOREWORD

After a decade of getting to know Blanca, witnessing a small part of her journey, and being asked to write the foreword to her book, I'm reminded of what the esteemed Dominican writer Julia Alvarez wrote in her novel, _In the Time of Butterflies_, "A book is not, after all, a historical document, but a way to travel through the human heart." Blanca's story certainly reflects that sentiment.

Heart is what I think of when I close my eyes and reflect on the ten years of friendship and her support. As the President and CEO of the Hispanic Heritage Foundation—a national leadership organization which inspires, prepares and positions young leaders in the community, classroom and workforce—I want to focus on Blanca's passion for serving her community which I'm sure translates into her successful career.

I have the clear vision of Blanca compassionately speaking in Spanish with the humble parents of high-achieving but under-served youngsters. I have the vision of

Blanca hugging the students and the look on the students' faces as she talks them through her personal and career path to show them that anything is possible. I have the vision of Blanca being approached by students many years later and continuing to provide advice and resources as they enter the workforce. And I have visions of Blanca approaching me and asking if there is anything she can do beyond her role as a sponsor through her company in terms of volunteering with our organization.

Passing on blessings is at the very core of my friend Blanca. She takes the responsibility as a profoundly spiritual woman and Latina role model extremely seriously. She lives her life in a way which has allowed her to stand out and succeed in the corporate world as well as the community.

Any company will value someone who has no sense of entitlement, stays positive, looks out for her team, takes her work seriously, doesn't take herself too seriously, and uses common sense as she navigates the often complicated corporate waters. Yes, "street smarts" have a place in the sophisticated world of corporate America—and in the community.

Blanca's credibility as a role model starts and ends with her journey as an immigrant born in a small town, in the Dominican Republic, to being raised in New York City's public housing development, and 34 years as a professional working for a Fortune 5 company. Where she started, however, is who she is and wears proudly like a medallion. It is her DNA, and it is her inspiration. It is also why she has had the impact she has had on so many, especially parents and students who are looking for trusted successful Latinos and role models.

With the high school graduation rate for Latinos just above 50 percent and 12 percent for Latinos to graduate from college, our community is in considerable need of not only inspiration but a clear path for overcoming obstacles and a blueprint for a productive life. I applaud her company for providing Blanca with a tremendous platform from which to deliver her salient message. And I applaud the publishers of this book for allowing her to tell her story, which will resonate with a vast audience. And most importantly, demonstrate that anything is possible.

José Antonio Tijerino, *President and CEO*
—Hispanic Heritage Foundation

About the Hispanic Heritage Foundation

The Hispanic Heritage Foundation (HHF) is a 501c3, nonprofit which inspires, identifies, prepares and positions Latino leaders in the classroom, community and workforce to meet America's priorities. HHF also provides Latinos in America with role models, cultural pride and a promising future through public awareness campaigns and special events. What distinguishes HHF from other organizations is their focus on not simply helping a Latino but helping a Latino and a hundred more. With that as inspiration, HHF has developed a unique pipeline of 75,000 vetted, energized emerging Latino leaders. Please visit www.HispanicHeritage.org.

INTRODUCTION

Who says you can't climb the corporate ladder—your boss, your coworkers, your parents' or siblings' negative programming?

How do you excel when the odds are overwhelmingly stacked against you every step of the way?

How does an immigrant, born in a small town, in the Dominican Republic, and raised in New York City's public housing development, wind up in a Fortune 5 corporation?

My son once told me that a person from the South Bronx once asked him, "What does your mother do for a living?"

He responded, "She is a businesswoman at Mobil."

The person responded, "People like us do not get jobs like that."

Well, they do, and I did by empowering myself and creating an amazing career. I did so by not letting the naysayers get me down and by believing in myself and my abilities.

I entered the corporate world while still working on my undergraduate degree and after six years in a small law firm. At that time, there were no role models, no one to emulate, no one to offer advice on the dos and don'ts of the corporate environment, so I had to do it my way. I had to learn things on my own by trial and error, making a lot of mistakes along the way. Some of these mistakes caused me some career moves, and others I was able to overcome.

Many new employees in the corporate environment lack direction, especially those young people straight out of college or university. The informal education of navigating the corporate environment happens on the job by trial and error.

Empower Yourself for an Amazing Career is written for the millions of women recently entering the corporate environment, providing guidance that they may not get in the classroom or at home.

It is written for the millions who are in need of guidance and advice on how to advance their careers and move on after career failure or dealing with a bad, ineffective manager. Millions of employees are silently suffering through the abuse of a bad manager or are depressed about their inability to advance their careers.

My goal is to provide guidance and encouragement to those new to the corporate environment and those who may be feeling stuck in their careers and want to continue to grow, expand, and be successful.

This book is honest and pragmatic in its accounts of my thirty-four-year experience and provides sound advice based on my reality, my personal experience. It features practical advice on how to manage conflict, tips on getting ahead, navigating the land mines and banana peels in the corporate world, and overcoming career failure.

The overarching message of this book is to inspire and motivate readers to forge ahead, no matter what trials and tribulations they encounter along the road to success.

The overall tone is positive, uplifting, inspiring, and motivational, while at the same time realistic. It encourages readers to dare to dream and prepare and position themselves for that next promotion.

The following pages contain information about personal career mistakes, guidance beneficial to anyone who dreams of building a successful career. Personal stories are paired with strategies for overcoming adversity in the workplace.

You will discover how to assess the journey of your career, how to manage a bad manager, how to deal with career failure, and how to develop a career road map with uplifting and inspiring advice.

Empower Yourself for an Amazing Career offers a fresh approach and insight on climbing the corporate ladder, combining practical, common-sense advice with inner wisdom and spirituality, providing strategies to increase the chances of success in the workplace.

CHAPTER 1

YOUR CAREER—A JOURNEY, NOT A DESTINATION

How do you define career success? Is it becoming a CEO (Chief Executive Officer), making it to middle or senior management, reaching a certain income level, or getting that corner office?

If you define career success by your job title, your position within the organization, or where you end up at the end of your career, then you are missing the point of your career experience.

Your career is not defined by where you end up; it is not a destination. Your career is a *journey* that is assessed by your integrity, how you traveled that road, the stops you made along the way, the people you met and inspired to reach their full potential, and the lessons you learned. Those lessons brought you full circle, making you not only the person you are today but also the one you will grow into tomorrow.

The journey of your career is defined by your choices, actions, reactions, and inactions in light of the opportunities and challenges life presents to you. At its core your career success is about your self-evaluation, your sense of accomplishment, and your ability to define success for yourself, rather than letting others define it for you.

I am about to introduce you to an extremely powerful person. This person will be your travel partner, providing all of the guidance and tools you need, along the journey of your career, to empower yourself to transform your *job* into an amazing *career*. This person is your *inner self*.

Life is about free will, options, and choices; and no one but you can determine the ultimate path of your career. Ultimately, your accomplishments and the realization of your dreams are up to you, because you can be all that your inner self has in store for you.

Only you can access what is inside of you, bring it forward, and make it a reality. Your inner self has the ability to visualize and realize an amazing career, because your true potential far exceeds what you have tapped into thus far. You can draw that full potential forward by focusing on your strengths and abilities.

Intellectual, academic knowledge can help us up to a certain point by providing information that will help us evaluate different options. However, we always seem to have a need to satisfy our inner voice by making sure that the decisions we make are directly aligned with our inner guidance. When our decisions are not aligned with our inner guidance, we get the nagging voice second-guessing our decisions and motives.

As you assess the journey of your career, you will look to various independent sources for guidance: your spouse, friends, family, co-workers, mentors—and even your boss. However, because of their differing backgrounds and life experiences, the advice you receive from each may conflict and be confusing to you as you strive to make informed career decisions.

Listen to all of the well-intentioned advice and gauge it with *your* intuition, your gut feelings. When it is right for you, it will ring true in your heart and your gut. Take what works for you and leave the rest behind. Ultimately, you have to learn to trust your inner self—your inner compass— to help you build a solid foundation for a rewarding career, to help you move through significant transitions and barriers, and to point you in the direction of your next step—the next path that will lead you to that next plateau.

As you continue to travel patiently down your chosen path, the road may seem long, winding, and never-ending and realizing your dreams may seem daunting, overwhelming, and, at times, elusive. It may be difficult to remain optimistic when you see no evidence of your dreams coming to fruition. However, you must continue to believe in yourself, regardless of negative circumstances and input from those around you.

Your dreams may require time, energy, and other action on your part before they materialize. Stay positive, be optimistic, and keep plugging away at your main goals. Chances are you are doing much better than you think and success is most likely just around the corner.

Do not let your boss, your coworkers, or your parents' or siblings' negative programming make you lose your self-esteem or self-worth. Unfortunately, whether intentional or not, some relationships shape and ingrain a negative reflection of self into our consciousness through years of disappointments, uncertainties, and doubts. These negative reflections tend to stay with us and develop our overall impression of ourselves and life as a whole, limiting our experiences to what our ego-based fears allow.

The ego is shallow and fear-based, and its primary focus is all about "me". With this ego-based focus, you are bound to fail, making your worst fears come true. Ego-based fears can be extremely powerful and control your mind. If your self-image is threatened, the ego diligently goes to work by partnering with fear to create a pattern of fearful thoughts, perceptions, and ideas.

The ego's role is to help you clearly understand your individual needs, values, and goals in life, constantly reminding you who you are supposed to be. As such, it is constantly evaluating and manipulating fear-based emotions such as inadequacy, humiliation, and failure. These fear-based emotions can drown you in a pool of your own negativity, as your thoughts remind you over and over again of your weaknesses, powerlessness, and hopelessness.

It is destructive to indulge in self-pitying thoughts and emotions, so take the time to understand and resolve all insecurities. Stop being your own worst enemy and harshest critic.

When you feel inadequate and useless, you sometimes start to attract circumstances, relationships, and situations that affirm that belief. Your body language will confirm your thoughts, and others will perceive your vulnerability and treat you as someone who doesn't deserve respect and can be pushed around. Body language makes up between 60-90% of your daily responses. Whether you're aware of it or not, when you interact with others, you're continuously giving and receiving wordless signals. Replace those old insecurities and fears with new empowering thoughts, and reclaim your self-worth and self-esteem so that you can realize the success you deserve.

Learning to accept and re-affirm your position in life and remold your thoughts will end your self-sabotaging behavioral patterns. New, empowering thoughts will yield the benefit of knowing that life has equipped you with everything you need to succeed.

Stop looking into the rearview mirror of your life, and leave your hurts and insecurities behind. Look straight ahead with your head held high. Get excited about your goals and where you want to go in your career and life will assert all that you deserve to be and do.

Your career should be about growing, expanding your horizons, and surfing on the cutting edge of your industry and environment. While, in the midst of your career, you may arrive at plateaus where you will rest, slowing down and taking it easy as you celebrate your accomplishments and success, but the time will come when you will be ready to move on and do more. For every milestone, you reach in your career; there is always that next level beyond it that will take you to even greater career satisfaction.

Sometimes, career satisfaction can be found in mentoring others—in giving back. Take the time to invest in someone else. All it takes is a few minutes of your time to help others navigate their careers.

On the journey of your career, I encourage you to take the time to give back, to "pay it forward," and to make a positive difference in the life of someone who can learn from your experience. You will be amazed at how it will positively impact your life and your career. True success can at times be defined as having reached back to help others achieve their full potential and career goals.

When assessing your career, remember that it is a journey and not a destination; a journey that will be defined by the decisions you made along the way.

Your career is a journey; so why not make it an *amazing* journey worth taking.

"*Life is the sum of your choices.*"—*Albert Camus*

Chapter 2

The Corporate Culture—
Is it for You?

Corporations, like people, have distinct personalities, and no amount of hard work and determination will help you get ahead if you are in the wrong corporate culture. The culture of an organization is its personality, its core values and beliefs that can affect your career satisfaction and success. The culture can evolve over time as a result of hiring new people or revamping the senior management team.

It is essential to ensure that you fit into the corporate culture as it can make an enormous difference in your interactions, attitude, and happiness. Select a company that fits your goals and needs. Weigh the pros and cons of working with both small and large organizations.

Small companies tend to have fewer than five hundred employees. They tend to be fast-paced, and this can make it easier to excel on the job; employees have the opportunity to get involved in a variety of projects and gain well-rounded experience. When working with a small company, you can be a "big fish in a small pond," with a much better chance of being recognized through your daily interactions with senior management. This interaction can go a long way toward getting the decision-makers to know you and your abilities and aspirations. If you are a strong performer, you are likely to get faster promotions and pay raises.

In a large corporation, you are "a small fish in the ocean." Large corporations tend to have two thousand or more employees competing to climb the corporate ladder to reach the limited number of positions at the very top.

Career opportunities within a large corporation are boundless. You have the opportunity to learn, grow, and expand your horizons, all within the same company. On the other hand, the large corporate world can be "dog-eat-dog." This survival-of-the-fittest environment can be even more extreme if you work at the corporate headquarters.

Many people choose to work at large corporations for the benefits and job security. Large companies provide a stable work environment, and the growth of the company largely depends on the team spirit of the workforce.

Larger companies tend to offer a higher starting salary as compared to smaller companies. However, large companies offer less flexibility as they tend to operate in a more structured manner, and salary increments, bonuses, and promotions are usually linked to your individual performance, the financial performance of the company, and in some instances the results of "forced ranking". Forced ranking is a somewhat controversial tool utilized by large organizations to identify a company's best and worst performing employees, using person-to-person comparisons. The objective of the forced ranking is to segregate the workforce into three tiers: the top 20 percent represent the future leaders, the middle 70 percent are consistently solid performers, and the bottom 10 percent represent those that are perceived to contribute the least.

Large corporations encourage continuous learning by providing a variety of training programs designed to develop and sharpen your skills and technical knowledge of the industry.

Since many of these large corporations have a broad national and sometimes international network, you have the potential to relocate to your favorite destination. You may also get the opportunity to travel to countries you would probably not make an effort (or could not afford) to visit.

When deciding on where you will eventually work, keep in mind that you will most likely spend more time with your coworkers than with your biological or nuclear family. Your place of employment will become your home away from home; your coworkers will become your extended family. Unlike your biological or nuclear family, you can choose the people and the environment you work in. So make sure that you fit in the environment and that it is a place where you can visualize yourself flourishing in a rewarding and successful career.

The importance of ensuring that your personal values are aligned with your employers' cannot be underestimated as this alignment will directly impact and influence your productivity, satisfaction, and opportunities within the company.

I've seen many people throughout the years who did not have this alignment. As such, they found themselves in a situation where the work appeared to be much harder than what it truly was; they hated their jobs, and were utterly miserable as they were constantly striving to be something they were not. In the process, they lost their sense of self and identity.

As you assess your company or a prospective employer, make sure you fully understand the environment and culture you are seeking. Make sure the company's core values are directly aligned with your own. If they are not, chances are, you will not achieve your career goals and aspirations.

In some cases, the culture is implied, but in others, there are formal standards that define the corporate ethics, beliefs, and expected behavior of employees.

As in our society, ethical behavior is a common expectation in the corporate world. Employees are expected to conduct business in an ethical manner, always recognizing what is right and wrong. In both cases, it is your responsibility to distinguish between right and wrong. Learning that distinction in your corporate environment is extremely critical, as failure to do so can cost you your career or job.

Some corporations have zero tolerance for unethical behavior, and ignorance of the law, rule, or regulation is no excuse. Employees are expected to conduct themselves and business in a way that positively impacts the reputation of the company, the bottom line, and the stakeholders who have a vested interest in the corporation.

Employees and shareholders also expect their CEO and executives to behave and manage the company in an ethical manner. For example, the executives at Enron were greedily only thinking of themselves, without concern for any responsibility to its employees and stockholders, which resulted in the implosion of the company. Management's unethical behavior ruined the lives of many employees and stockholders. Enron is not alone; there have been other corporations that found themselves in trouble for unethical and illegal behavior.

Such behavior erodes the confidence of the public, employees, and stockholders. It also makes the public skeptical about the ethics of corporate America. It creates an overall distrust, as the public thinks, "*What else are they hiding? How many others are out there duping the public, their employees, and stakeholders?*"

Creating and sustaining an ethical environment is a long and continuous journey in both your personal behavior and how you conduct business. So, if there is even a hint of impropriety in a proposed action, stop and rethink your position before proceeding.

In addition to asking the basic benefits questions when assessing your company or prospective employer, ask yourself the follow questions:

- Can I see myself in this environment for the next five, ten, or fifteen years?
- Does this company appreciate its employees and their contributions?
- Does the company offer ample opportunities for career development and upward mobility?

- What is the proportion of women and minorities in leadership positions and what is their role?
- What behaviors are rewarded and frowned upon?
- Do I agree with the company's ethics?
- Is the corporate structure too stifling?
- Will I succeed in a formal or an informal environment; a small company versus a large corporation?

Take the time to evaluate your prospective or current organization to ensure that you fully understand the culture. You must ensure that the values and culture of the company are directly aligned with your own, so you can flourish in a rewarding and successful career.

"If you do not manage culture, it manages you, and you may not even be aware of the extent to which this is happening."—Edgar Schein, Professor MIT School of Management

CHAPTER 3

MANAGING A BAD MANAGER

Abusive, nasty, obnoxious people exist in every facet of life. They are in every company and industry. They are in our families, neighborhoods, and workplaces. These people can easily wear you out, frustrate you, and make your life miserable. They are bullying, intrusive, and controlling; and will rarely provide constructive feedback. They are glory hogs who will take credit for your work and will not support you during a crisis.

Dictionary.com defines the word power as "the possession of control or command over others". These managers let the power of their leadership position go to their heads; and as a result, they do not use their power, they abuse it which results in coercive and bullying behavior. Managers have a choice to use or abuse the power they have been given by the organization. Sadly, too many choose to abuse that power.

Many of us have experienced working under a bad manager. Bad managers are not limited to just the abusive, bullying type. They can also be control freaks that micromanage and nitpick at everything you do. They can be paternalistic, managing their employees as if they were children. Making decisions on their own believing that they know what is in the best interest of the employees. They can be overbearing and condescending, giving feedback in an abusive and demoralizing fashion. They can be two-faced telling their employees one thing but behaving in a way that only benefits their own career. They set unreasonable levels of expectations for their staff. They can be non-supportive of their employees throwing them under the bus when things go wrong. They tend to have poor communication and leadership skills which results in a lack of guidance for the staff. These are just a few examples of some of the characteristics of a bad manager; the actual list can be quite extensive. I'm sure that you can name a few based on your experience and perspective.

One management style does not work for all employees and what may appear to be an appropriate approach for one person will not work for the next. However, there are some managers that everyone agrees are horrendous managers with zero interpersonal skills and no one quite understands how or why they are still managing people.

In fact, many employees have moved on to new companies or departments just to get away from a bad boss. The years of service for those that choose to walk away can vary as everyone's situation differs based on their tolerance and level of patience. They have walked away on a sour note feeling abused, over-worked, under-appreciated, and at times under-paid. Many walk away from good-paying jobs, excellent benefits, and even their pension all because of one bad manager. In these extreme cases, many employees feel so stressed that they leave to preserve their health and sanity. For most, it is the best decision they have ever made and the one regret is not having made the decision sooner.

There are others that have had their careers derailed or totally ruined by a bad manager but have chosen to stay with the company. Some stay hoping that they or their boss will be transferred or promoted out of the department. For some, it could be age, years of service, or the ability to duplicate their current salary, benefits package, and pension. People choose to stay for various reasons that are dependent on their particular situation, so the list can be quite extensive.

Unfortunately, this is a challenge that too many employees have to face on a daily basis. There is no single solution when deciding to quit or stick it out as each person's situation is unique. The final decision is a highly personal one that takes many factors into consideration. At the end of the day, you have to be satisfied with your choice and make the best decision you can under your particular situation. The key is to remain true to yourself and your goals.

Unless you are independently wealthy, chances are you can't do without your job. So, how do you defend yourself against the attacks of a bad manager while preserving your sanity, dignity, and career? How do you handle a bad manager that constantly undermines you and your abilities?

You must first accept the fact that your boss is in charge and managing your career, which makes the situation much harder to manage. It is a fact of your work life that you have to answer to your boss. If your intention is to develop and grow a career within the company, then you need to figure out a way to get along with your boss or learn to work around his less-than-supportive behavior.

So, instead of lashing out which in most cases will work against you, or lodging a complaint with your human resource department, maintain your professionalism and attempt to resolve the problem yourself. Some suggested strategies can include:

- Network; build relationships with other senior employees or managers so that they can get to know you and your abilities. Broadening your network will help thwart any negative feedback from your boss.

- Enhance your credibility by keeping up your work ethics, meeting your commitments and deadlines. Remain diligent in your daily duties. Do not give your boss anything that he can use against you. Try to be the perfect employee.

- Do not over-promise and under-deliver by taking on more responsibility than you can realistically handle. If you do not deliver on your commitments, your boss will most likely use this against you, regardless of your efforts and intentions.

- Fully understand the objectives of your work group and your manager's expectations by prioritizing your daily tasks or projects. Review your prioritized to-do list with your boss to ensure that he agrees with your priorities.

Discussing and documenting your priorities will minimize the potential for misunderstanding on your deliverables.

- To the extent possible, minimize personal contact with your manager. Is it possible to communicate via e-mail or voice mail? Minimizing direct contact can potentially reduce the opportunity for confrontation with your boss.

- Kill him with kindness when he is most likely expecting to get a rise out of you. Disarm him with unexpected polite behavior; he'll be confused and unsure what to make of your reaction. Hopefully he will stop to think about what he has just said or done. Sometimes people say or do things for effect, to get a certain reaction out of you. Try not to give in to this manipulation of your psyche.

- Try to give your boss the benefit of the doubt. Do you believe that his actions are intentional or malicious? Or is he the kind of the person that just does not realize how he is coming across? Few people make an honest self-assessment of their behavior and without constructive feedback will continue to remain oblivious of their unprofessional and unsupportive behavior. A study based on surveys and interviews with 200 plus managers in approximately 40 countries concluded that most ineffective leaders remain blissfully unaware of the harm they do to their organizations. The study also found that overall only 35 percent of respondents at high performing companies said their leaders were doing a good job inspiring their teams. (Thunderbird School of Global Management *When bosses do harm: Breaking the hindrance trap,* by Kannan Ramaswamy, Ph.D., and Bill Youngdahl, Ph.D.)

- Try to assess the situation from all angles, including what you may have contributed to the situation. Then, take the high road with as much patience, perseverance, and professionalism as you can muster. This can be a daunting task that is much easier said than done.

  o Once you have fully assessed the situation take immediate steps to attempt to rectify the problem. Schedule a meeting with your boss to let him know in a professional manner your understanding of the situation. Prepare talking points for your meeting as this will ensure that you stay focused on the pertinent issues.

  o Address your concerns in a professional, polite, focused, and calm manner. Being rude and unprofessional is counterproductive and will not help you meet your goals and objectives. A frank, polite, and professional discussion can go a long way.

  o Addressing your concerns with your boss may also backfire and make things worse. However, instead of sitting on the sidelines silently suffering from his abusive behavior, you should at least attempt to address the situation. At least you will have the satisfaction of knowing that you took actionable steps to remedy the situation instead of being a victim.

You never know how someone is going to react, and you may just be pleasantly surprised. Most people carry around their own fears, weaknesses, and idiosyncrasies; and given the opportunity, most will try to do better. Your boss may just walk away with renewed respect for you for having the courage to stand up for yourself in a professional manner.

In some cases, you will have to agree to disagree, and that is okay too.

If, on the other hand, the problem you are facing is of a more serious nature and you believe human resource intervention is required, then you may want to document the situation. Documenting your situation means writing down all of the details and retaining any memos, letters, e-mails, or voice mails that can support your position. This documentation is essential for filing grievances should the difficulty of your situation escalate and require a paper trail to support your position in a formal hearing.

- Fully document, in chronological order, all of the relevant factors that support your position, while the facts are fresh in your mind.
- Use full names of all involved and include any potential witnesses that can support your position.
- Stick to the facts by focusing on *who, what, where,* and *when*. Resist the temptation, to speculate on *why* the situation occurred.
- Consult a lawyer, if necessary.

Going up against management or the company should not be taken lightly. The formal grievance process can be a daunting task that can be extremely stressful and difficult to endure. However, you will increase your chances of prevailing if you present a well-supported, objectively-written, and thoroughly documented case in your defense.

Difficult work situations ebb and flow in intensity so assess your situation and take the appropriate action steps warranted by the circumstances.

If after your best efforts to resolve the issue, you see no evidence of improvement in your situation, and you still want to stay with the company, you may want to consider transferring out of your department, as a last resort. If you decide to transfer, do not bad-mouth your manager or peers to your replacement or new colleagues. Try not to burn any bridges. Leave with as much dignity and honor as you can muster by honoring your commitments to your department before you leave.

While you probably cannot change a bad manager, the good news is that you can learn from a bad boss. You can learn how *not* to manage. You can learn how to recognize inappropriate behavior. You have a living, breathing example of how a bad manager behaves. This is behavior you do not want to emulate. As a leader, you want to use not abuse the power you have been granted.

Deciding to learn something from a difficult situation is the best strategy for coping with adversity. Ask yourself what you can learn from this situation. People will come in and out of your life for a specific purpose. Try not to miss the lesson and the growth opportunity that life has provided you through this relationship and experience.

Regard everyone you meet as a co-star in the movie of your career. Every stage of your journey has helped you become stronger, wiser, more patient, resilient, and experienced. Your current situation is simply another stage that brings an opportunity to learn and continue growing.

So, instead of being this bad manager's victim, become his apprentice. Take control by choosing to make the adverse situation part of your informal education.

When someone's behavior triggers so much anguish, you may hold resentment toward that person, maybe even daydreaming of how to get even. I know I spent many days thinking how I could get even with an abusive manager, but in the end, logic prevailed, and he remained unharmed.

Holding on to resentment makes you an emotional hostage to the other person, as it consumes your energy, enthusiasm, and effectiveness. These people tend to be unhappy in their own lives, and it is often said that misery loves company.

Don't allow yourself to become an emotional hostage. I spent many years hating an abusive manager, and honestly it was not worth it. I wish I'd had someone to counsel and coach me on the art of forgiving and letting go.

Forgive the person, let go of the resentment, let it roll off of your back, and walk away. Letting go will free you from the hostage situation. The benefits derived from forgiving will be a much better option than harboring resentment and suffering any adverse consequence as a result of acting rashly or in revenge. It is not worth the time and energy such people require. Let it go, and be free of the mental hold this person has imposed. If you do not let go, you will remain trapped in your own world of misery.

Rocky Start to My Corporate Career

I started my corporate career in 1982 at the age of twenty-five after working as a legal secretary in Midtown Manhattan for six years. I had been married for seven years, had three young children, and I was still working on my Undergraduate degree in International Business Management at Pace University.

My family immigrated to the United States in 1963 from the Dominican Republic, and the first 18 years of my life were spent in a predominantly Spanish-speaking environment. Most of the students in my elementary and high schools, the local businesses, and friends were of Hispanic descent. There was little to no exposure to other cultures. However, I did not understand the impact of this lack of diversity until I ventured into the working world of Midtown Manhattan. Despite some of the similarities in my background with the other secretaries at the law firm, I seem to have missed a lot in the translation while growing-up in New York City's Public Housing Development. I had a lot of catching up to do.

In high school, we were taught to master the art of shorthand, typing, and developing business correspondence but they failed to teach us about dress code, office politics, how to answer a business phone, and other professional protocols. When I think back at the group of girls who graduated with me, very few, if any, were ready to enter the work force. We were all a bit rough around the edges.

After High School, I entered an all-girls nine month co-op secretarial program in midtown Manhattan. This program was an excellent way to ease into the professional world of midtown Manhattan. The program allowed me to attend school half of the time and work the other half at Marine Midland Bank corporate offices.

The secretarial co-op program focused on teaching students how to dress and behave professionally in an office setting; something I was in dire need of. We were required to wear skirts, something Blanca, the tomboy, did not even own. My attire growing up was strictly jeans and sneakers. None of that girlie-girl stuff for me.

I had excellent hands-on skills, typing 120 words per minute, taking dictation at approximately 140 words per minute and all of the protocols of crafting, developing, and producing business communication. However, I knew absolutely nothing about office politics, protocol, and professional office etiquette. I did not even know how to properly answer a business telephone call in a professional manner. I did extremely well in the classroom environment, but I failed miserably at the job with the bank. I was way out of my league. I was not ready for the corporate environment.

At the conclusion of the co-op program, Marine Midland did not offer me a job. At the time, I did not fully understand why. I later recognized that the bank was looking for someone who was a bit more sophisticated, and they fully recognized that I was not ready for the corporate environment. When I graduated from secretarial school, I was a bit more refined, but I still had a long, long way to go.

Fortunately, the secretarial school had a job-placement program, and in June 1976, I got a job with a small law firm that specialized in corporate litigation. The law firm was not looking for finesse; they were looking for someone with above average intelligence who could type, take dictation, and file.

Fortunately, life has a way of directing our steps in such a way that we end up exactly where we need to be at each stage of our lives. The environment at the law firm was conducive to learning how to polish some of the rough edges without being judgmental. I learned about this other world from the other secretaries and lawyers who grew up in middle- to upper-middle-class environments. Not only was I learning social etiquette and behavior, I was learning a lot about corporate law and proceedings.

At the law firm, we worked long hours. It was common to work from 9:30 a.m. to sometime the next morning. We were constantly busy providing a wide range of secretarial, administrative, and office-management duties, such as typing or revising legal briefs, taking dictation, transcribing from recorded dictation, filing, and whatever other tasks that may have arisen as a result of the firm's case load. One of my other official duties included managing the medical insurance policy for those who worked at the firm. This duty required that I fully understand all of the benefits provided to all of the employees. In other words, the firm did not have a human resources department, so we all had mini human-resource responsibilities. The secretaries were also required to have a notary public license, since we would have to notarize the lawyers' signatures on documents to be filed with the court. The State of New York holds notaries public to a high standard, and first-time candidates are required to pass a state-proctored exam with questions taken from the New York Notary Public License law booklet. Knowledge of all aspects of the notary license law, legal terms, and duties of the notary public are tested on this exam.

After two years of working as a legal secretary, I looked around and realized that there was no room for growth. Somehow, I knew that this was not what I was meant to do in life. I realized that there was more to life than just making a living. I was making a great salary at the law firm, but it was a dead-end job. Unless one attended law school, the highest position one could hope to attain at a small law firm was head secretary, office manager, or paralegal.

So I decided to get a college education and embarked on the road to my undergraduate degree. After the decision to go back to school was solidified, I realized that I couldn't afford the tuition. I was not going to let this minor issue deter me from my desire to obtain a college education. So I negotiated an agreement with the partners at the law firm, whereby they would advance the money for tuition at the beginning of the semester, and I would repay the loan by working overtime. Working overtime was a necessity at the law firm and not all of the secretaries were always willing or available to do so. By agreeing to serve as the overtime stand-in, I was meeting a need in the firm in exchange for tuition advancement. I was extremely grateful for the interest-free loan and the generosity extended by the partners.

Two years into my college education, I decided that I needed to get some corporate experience. At Pace University, I met another student who knew that I was interested in getting a job in the corporate environment.

She advised that there was a vacant secretarial position in her company and that I should apply. Working as a secretary in a major corporation was an excellent way to explore and discover the inner workings of the corporate environment. So I decided to apply and get a glimpse of the corporate world. I interviewed with the human resource department, the business line manager and was hired on the spot.

The six years I spent at the law firm were my formative years. The office was my home away from home, and the people became part of my extended family. Leaving the law firm was one of the hardest things I've had to do. I started out at the young age of nineteen, naïve, childless, and rough around the edges. I left at the age of twenty-five, much more poised, refined, and with three children. I still had some maturing and polishing to achieve, but my smarts, skills, work ethics, and talents compensated for my lack of tact.

This was a significant turning point in my life. I felt like the little bird that ultimately has to leave its nest and venture the world on its own.

I took a substantial cut in pay to acquire the corporate experience. I viewed this cut in pay as a short-term loss in order to obtain a long-term gain. As a result of this cut in pay, I had to continue working at the law firm part time, in order to make ends meet and to repay the money loaned to me by the firm for tuition. It took me approximately one full year to repay my debt to the law firm and re-adjust my budget to the decreased income.

The difference between the corporate environment and a small firm is like night and day. The law firm was small with approximately twenty employees and offered a nurturing familial environment. The corporate world, on the other hand, was immense, and one I knew absolutely nothing about. I was like a fish out of water and not sure this red tape and bureaucratic environment was for me. Fortunately, the law firm had left its doors open for me, and I always had the option to go back if things did not work out.

The secretarial job with the corporation was extremely basic in its duties, not at all challenging, and frankly dull. Notwithstanding the mundane assignment, there were a couple of significant benefits to having a less demanding full-time job. One benefit was the ability to do my school work during the day. In this position, I was able to complete my work and help the other secretaries with their work in a matter of hours. As a result of getting my required reading or assignments completed during the work day, I was able to use my free time to spend with my family. One other significant advantage was the tuition reimbursement offered by the corporation which eased the financial burden of tuition. As a result, I was able to take as many classes as I could handle, instead of only taking what I could afford.

Despite these benefits, my corporate experience got off to a rocky start. In addition to struggling with balancing a budget, taking care of a family, and being a part-time college student, I was assigned to work for a less than supportive, abusive manager. I was told that secretaries from the temp agencies would come in the morning and not return after lunch. He had exhausted the internal pool of available secretaries, so the human resource department was compelled to hire from outside of the company.

On more than one occasion, I saw a different person walking out of his office in tears. In fact, one of the professional women in our group, who was in the United States on foreign assignment, quit the company because of his abusive behavior. From what I could surmise, senior management was aware of this abusive behavior and did absolutely nothing about it. In fact, they seemed to reward him with one promotion after another. It appeared to me that what truly mattered to the management at the time were the results, regardless of how people were being treated. Everyone seemed to be ignoring his less than professional behavior. When it came to the business and producing results, this man was extremely knowledgeable and savvy. If only he had been as effective at managing his interpersonal skills.

Change is a certainty in life, and that includes the workplace. The corporate environment is just like the weather; if you wait long enough, things will change. So try to weather the storm as best you can.

Fortunately for me and my sanity, this horrendous situation lasted a little less than six months, as senior management promoted the abusive manager to his next assignment of terror. However, before he left our department, he recommended my termination at the end of the six-month probationary period.

The quality of my work was not the issue; it was that I had the audacity to stand up to him and not tolerate his abusive behavior. If he pushed me, I pushed back harder. I'd go toe to toe with him, and he was not accustomed to anyone standing up to him, especially not a low-level secretary who had just walked through the door, such as myself. He hated that I dared to defend myself and that I would not let him break my spirit and resolve.

He once said to me, "You are wasting your time by going to Pace University and thinking that you are going to go up even one rung of the corporate ladder. I will make sure that no one in this company touches you with a ten-foot pole."

I responded, "This Company is not the only one hiring."

I have no idea what he told the manager who replaced him, but I got the distinct impression that the man was a bit apprehensive as I approached to introduce myself. Whatever he said to the new manager did not work. This new manager and I got along exceptionally well. In fact, he was extremely impressed with my skills and work ethic and became one of my biggest supporters and one of my informal mentors.

After the six-month probationary period, with the unwavering support of my manager, I became an official employee. Things were starting to look brighter. The dark cloud that had followed me was suddenly lifted.

I could now start working on a plan to achieve my first goal: to get out of the secretarial position. This was not commonplace, especially for someone new to the organization. I could honestly have retired five years earlier if I had a dime for every time I was told I was wasting my time by working toward my bachelor's degree. Many claimed that the company would never recognize a part-time degree, work efforts, or give me the opportunity to move out of the secretarial position. I did not let that discourage me. In fact, I saw it as a challenge.

I knew that getting ahead in this corporate environment was not going to be easy, but I was determined to put in the time required to get ahead.

> *"The secret to success is to start from scratch and keep on scratching."*
> **—Dennis Green**

CHAPTER 4

A HOLISTIC APPROACH TO YOUR CAREER

Upward mobility in any organization requires that you take a holistic approach to your career. A college education will get you hired, but getting ahead requires that you are well-rounded. So you must complement that formal education with informal education. You need to understand and abide by those unwritten and unspoken rules and regulations that are part of the corporate environment and that are required in order to get ahead.

I have seen many MBA graduates from the top business schools in the United States fail to succeed in the corporate environment. An MBA degree will get you in the door, but once you are in, you have to prove and distinguish yourself from the competition. You have to be able to demonstrate that you can contribute to the company's bottom line.

Succeeding in business requires a complete package that takes more than just a degree. Your experiences, skills, and abilities need to be varied and balanced; and determining which is more beneficial to a successful career, book smarts or street smarts, is exceptionally difficult, because it depends on the person and the circumstances.

You may know people who are book smart but do not have one ounce of common sense and are clueless as to how to survive in the real world. Others have the street smarts but do not know how to transfer or utilize those skills outside of their own environment.

Those with a combination of education, job experience, and street smarts, with experience as the key ingredient, are the ones who are likely to be most successful. Unfortunately, many corporations do not sufficiently value institutional knowledge and work experience when making career decisions. As a result, even if an employee has an excellent track record and has done exceptionally well in their job evaluations, when competing for a promotion or position with an MBA graduate, the credentials and luster of an MBA from a top business school will most likely win out.

An MBA from any university is an excellent credential to have and, all things being equal, may give you the edge you need to prevail when competing for a job or promotion. So, depending on your industry and if you have the time, stamina, energy, and willingness, get that MBA, even if it is part time, so that the next time education is the tiebreaker, you are the one with the edge to prevail.

A formal education is the individual's ticket in the door. However, the progression of their career and candidacy for a job or promotion should be measured by a combination of factors such as the number of years of work experience, accomplishments, results, and future potential.

We can distort the issues when we advocate that certain employees cannot get promoted or given the opportunity to showcase their talent because they do not have an advanced degree. However, the work experience, hands-on institutional knowledge that employees acquire during their years of service is extremely valuable. You will long forget the case studies and other material, but the hands-on experience is likely to stay with you for an exceedingly long time, in some cases forever.

Over my thirty-four-year career, I have learned that there are certain attributes, skills, and action steps which are essential to career success and better positioning yourself for that next career move.

In this chapter, I have detailed the top-ten items that I have found to be most critical when taking a holistic approach to your career. My top-ten items are not listed in order of importance, is in no way meant to be all-inclusive or work for everyone. This list may differ from one person to the other depending on their individual background and industry. This selection is based on my reality and experience. I encourage you to take and adhere to the items that resonate with you and leave the rest behind.

1. Go Above and Beyond
2. Commit to Continuous Learning
3. Master your Current Assignment
4. Differentiate Yourself from the Competition
5. Improve your Communication Skills
6. Establish Yourself as a Leader
7. Get off the Fence
8. Find a Mentor
9. Network
10. Project Confidence

1. Go Above and Beyond

Go above and beyond your current assignment by taking the initiative to volunteer even if no one asks you to do so. Volunteer to take on new responsibilities. However, before you volunteer always make sure that you have the time and resources to complete the assignment in a timely, professional manner never compromising the quality of your work.

Early in my career, I learned that quality is just as or more important than quantity. In one of my many work groups, there was a gentleman that had an extremely light workload compared to others in the group. When senior management was asked how it was possible that this person could get away with doing so little in comparison to what others were producing, he responded, "It is true that he does very little, but the little he does, he does extremely well." Lesson learned quality over quantity; never underestimate the value of producing an exceptional work product.

Always give people what they need, not just what the job description says your deliverable is. If somebody needs to look good in front of their boss, then that's your assignment. Think beyond the surface; think of the future benefits you can derive from helping others achieve their goals.

Taking the initiative to volunteer and help my group, worked extremely well for me early in my career. Once I became a permanent employee, my goal was to move out of the secretarial job and into one of the contract administration positions. At that time, our group was understaffed, and the analysts did not have sufficient time to run all of the required economics and spreadsheets. I took full advantage of this deficiency by volunteering to help out and, at the same time, it afforded me the opportunity to start learning the business.

I started out by simply entering data into the spreadsheets for the monthly economic report. Soon I had learned enough to support the group in running the actual economics and was no longer just entering data. I took the time to understand and learn the logic and fundamentals behind the numbers. I became so proficient at developing the economics that I was soon running the economics and developing the written reports myself. The operations analyst was simply reviewing and signing the final report.

My efforts did not go unnoticed by my department manager. He was so impressed by my ability to perform duties assigned to analysts at a much higher level that he lobbied to move me out of the secretarial job. He advocated that the corporation was not capitalizing on my skills and talents by keeping me in a secretarial position.

After two years, with a lot of hard work, determination, and a powerful mentor, I was given a promotion into the administrative group as a documentation specialist whose primary responsibility was preparing sales contracts for the crude-oil traders and the documentation associated with each cargo of crude oil.

I had managed to accomplish what many had said was not possible. I was promoted out of the secretarial realm into an administrative staff position prior to the completion of my formal education. My informal education and hard work were already working for me. A two-group promotion from a secretarial position into the administrative group was rare and a considerable milestone.

Take the time to learn the goals and objectives of your department. Keep abreast of what's going on and be on the lookout for deficiencies. Once you have identified a deficiency or opportunity, take the time to document your findings, propose a potential solution, and volunteer your time to help close the gap or capitalize on the opportunity. Reporting a problem without a solution is usually not well received. Thinking through a potential solution and volunteering your time to help resolve a problem or capitalize on an opportunity will assert your position as a reliable, dependable employee who takes initiative and is capable of handling a leadership role.

Opportunities to showcase your talent will not always be directly presented or offered to you by your management. There will be times when you have to take matters into your own hands by taking the initiative to find opportunities to showcase your talent. At times, this may be the only way to prove that you can contribute to the bottom line of the organization and add value while simultaneously enhancing and developing new skills.

Going above and beyond your daily duties or performing a task that is reserved for those at a much higher level than your current assignment is an excellent way to demonstrate your abilities, skills, strengths, leadership skills, and your desire to have a bigger role within the organization.

"If you're going to be truly successful, then set yourself apart from everyone else. Go beyond the limits of what

classifies the average person and be exceptional."
—Beyond the Quote—Motivational Business Quotes

2. Commit to Continuous Learning

Commit to continuous, informal and formal learning, growing as a person, and most importantly, learning from your mistakes. This commitment to continuous learning was the fundamental building block of my career.

I graduated from Pace University in 1985. I was physically and mentally exhausted and did not even attend my graduation. I felt that I had little in common with the other graduates. Most of the graduates were younger, single and had no children. I, on the other hand, was twenty-eight years old, married, and had three children. Looking back, I did not give myself sufficient credit for what I had just accomplished. I was glad to have obtained my bachelor's degree in international business management and grateful for the knowledge that I had acquired. Yet I still felt as though I was not yet finished.

So, in 1987, I enrolled in Pace's graduate program. I attended through August 1990, when Mobil moved its headquarters out of New York City. In 1991, I attempted to continue my graduate studies in Virginia, but transferring credits from Pace University was not as easy as I had hoped.

The university in Virginia would accept only a few of my credits, as the policy for getting a graduate degree from a certain university requires that the majority of the credits be obtained from that institution. This meant that I would have to forgo the three years-worth of credits I had earned with Pace University, literally starting my graduate studies from scratch. That was when I decided that I was done with my formal education.

My career was progressing nicely, and I felt that with my practical business experience, I probably did not need to complete the graduate degree program.

Early in my career, I committed to enhancing my formal education with informal education because I truly believed that this combination was going to be my ticket to a successful career with the company. I read all of the periodicals I could get my hands on so I could learn how the energy industry worked, how our company fit into the industry, and more importantly, how my current position fit into the bigger picture.

Being well-rounded and well-read will take you far, as you will be well-versed and can speak intelligently on various topics. Stay on top of what is going on in your industry and understand how it can be affected by legislation, local events, or other world matters.

Reading can open up your creative mind to new ideas and manner of thinking. It will expand your vocabulary and knowledge and may trigger an innovative idea to improve a work process.

Learning a new skill, technology, or process related to your industry—whether it is on-the-job training or class at your community college or business school—makes you smarter and increases your value as a person and an employee. You can take a course at a local school, university, executive management program, or any other organization that provides training for professionals.

In today's world, there are many options to choose from when pursuing an education. You do not have to take time out of your busy schedule to travel to a university. You can take online classes, which are extremely convenient for full-time employees, as they are readily accessible and can be done anytime and anyplace.

My personal favorites were the on-the-job training courses offered by our company. I took advantage of and exhausted all training opportunities the company provided. On-the-job training is usually free for the employee and can be taken during your workday. The training offered by your company is usually information or a skill set that your company perceives to be valuable to the company's viability. Many corporations not only welcome but encourage employees to take full advantage of these opportunities.

These training courses can range from technical to computer software skills. The main objective is to make sure you have the skill set required to get that next promotion. So check out your company's training courses. Invest the time, clear your schedule, and make time to take some training courses. This is one of the best ways to increase your net worth within your organization.

Regardless of which venue you choose, continuous learning is one of the best ways to further your career growth. No matter what stage of your career you are at, never stop learning. There is always a need to grow your knowledge base, improve, or learn a new skill. Technology and software are constantly being updated, and you must always strive to stay on top of the latest software required by your industry.

Committing to continuous learning keeps you engaged and challenged in your job and career.

"Education is the passport to the future, for tomorrow belongs to those who prepare for it today."
—Malcolm X

"Learning is a weightless treasure you can always carry easily."
—Chinese Proverb, A Collection of Wisdom

3. Master Your Current Assignment

If you master your current assignment, it is likely that management will have confidence in your ability to achieve more. You should never undermine or underestimate a strong work ethic, because, at the end of the day, your managers are concerned with productivity and the bottom line. Your ability to make your boss look good is priceless.

Staying focused and mastering each assignment without worrying about the ones that would follow was my approach. I knew that I had to master my current assignment. I had to let that next assignment take care of itself as I demonstrated my abilities and continued to build on the knowledge of the previous assignment.

Focus on the now, on what is right in front of you by mastering your current assignment and building and capitalizing on the knowledge of the previous one. View each assignment as a building block that will solidify the foundation of your career and will help propel you forward to that next plateau.

Yesterday is in the past, and it is exactly where it belongs, behind you, and tomorrow is not here yet. You cannot hope for a perfect past, but you can certainly work on a much better tomorrow by developing the skills and knowledge required for that next assignment today.

Take it one step at a time and celebrate each and every accomplishment along the way. Give yourself credit for a job well done.

I worked in the administration group for eight years, learning every aspect of the administrative part of the energy business. I learned the petroleum business from the ground up, and with each new assignment, I was building and capitalizing on the knowledge of the previous one. I viewed each assignment as a building block that solidified the foundation of my career and would help me achieve my goal to move out of the administration group.

My new goal to move into the supply operations group was not a common occurrence, and there were plenty of people saying it was impossible. These jobs were considered to be the threshold of the professional level within our organization. They were reserved for the incoming MBAs from Ivy League schools or the high flyers on foreign assignments. I did not have an Ivy League education; nor was I considered a high flyer at that time.

To make matters worse, in the mid to late '80s, the administration group I worked in was perceived to be the true "roach motel"—as in, "they check in, but they don't check out." The only way out was dying, retiring, or leaving the company to pursue other interests. The group carried a negative connotation of not being sufficiently professional. Getting a promotion out of the administration group and into supply and trading would be no easy feat.

From 1982 to 1992, every job I had done was clerical in nature and, although not sufficiently challenging, served as an excellent venue for learning the fundamentals of our industry. I spent the first ten years of my corporate career paying my dues and learning as much as I could about the energy business. My modus operandi was to be consistent in my performance. Then, work on increasing my responsibilities by mastering and capitalizing on each and every assignment, learning and thoroughly understanding the priorities of our business. No job was too big or small.

It did not matter to me that some of the assignments were not glorious; some were quite mundane, but I knew that even the smallest action within each assignment was educating and propelling me forward toward the next assignment and level.

In the early '90s, the company had a hiring freeze, and I was one of the beneficiaries. The company stopped hiring from the outside. As positions became available, the company was compelled to fill the vacancies from within. In 1992, I was promoted out of the Administration Group and into Supply and Trading. I was happy and grateful for the opportunity to showcase my talents and abilities by doing a supply operations job.

I finally had a job within the corporate environment that I considered challenging. I loved every minute of this stressful job, which brought with it a whole new set of challenges and opportunities.

Every time I moved up to the next level or a different department, there was always the culture and lingo to learn. This was the same company, yet the difference in the culture, mindset, and focus of the different groups never ceased to amaze me.

I had a lot of catching up to do if I wanted to compete with these high-powered MBA graduates from the top business schools in the United States, the high flyers, and others who had been in the industry for many years. I was smart and knew a lot about the business, but I still had a lot to learn.

This meant that I had to work twice as hard as everyone else to prove that I could do the job. It meant not letting anything slip and reading every single piece of paper that came across my desk. I was constantly researching and educating myself on how my job fit into the bigger scheme of things. I wanted to make sure that I was making a difference and contributing to the bottom line.

"If a man is called to be a street sweeper, he should sweep streets even as Michelangelo painted, or Beethoven composed music, or Shakespeare wrote poetry. He should sweep streets so well that all the hosts of heaven and earth will pause to say, here lived a great street sweeper who did his job well."
—Martin Luther King, Jr.

"Yesterday is history, tomorrow is a mystery. And today? Today is a gift. That's why we call it the present."
—B. Olatunji

4. Differentiate Yourself from the Competition

Identify your unique and transferable skills and strengths. Define and refine your personal brand so that you can enhance your marketability. Find a way to differentiate yourself and stand out from the rest of the competition.

You are an individual, and there is no one else exactly like you. Your personal attributes are the things that distinguish and set you apart from your competition. So leverage your personal style, values, and talents, and don't be shy about self-promoting them. Toot your own horn. This is certainly not bragging; it is marketing this product called *You.*

Be your own campaign manager, and promote your most marketable and transferable skills, experiences, and expertise. You are in the best position to manage this campaign; if not you, then who? You know what you have to offer, what you bring to the table, so showcase it whenever you have the opportunity. Because not only is it essential for you to get to know people, but people need to get to know you.

Distinguish yourself by developing and mastering the skills required in your field and finding a niche or a need in your department that is not being met. Go above and beyond your job description, volunteer for special projects that will showcase your abilities. By doing so, you increase the likelihood of getting noticed and getting that next promotion or assignment.

Another way to distinguish yourself is to ensure that you adopt a professional appearance. There are no written dress code standards within most corporations; however, there are certain unwritten expectations. Anyone who aspires to progress within the corporate environment needs to understand the importance of personal appearance. You only get one chance to make the right first impression so don't blow it by ignoring your appearance.

Is it fair to judge a person's qualifications by what they wear? Of course, it is not. However, the reality is that most of us tend to judge people by their appearance. There is a time and a place for everything, and you need to ensure that you are properly dressed for your work environment. As campaign manager of your career, you are marketing that product called *You* to management and other decision makers, and you never know who is going to judge you by your attire.

Unfortunately, a woman's attire is much closer scrutinized than a man's. Men choose a shirt, tie, business suit, and they are done. Women, on the other hand, have many wardrobe alternatives, choices in attire, and combination of accessories. As a result, it is much more difficult for women to get it right. This is not to imply that men can get away with dressing unprofessional. However, it can be much easier for women to cross the line from professional to unprofessional attire.

The decisions you make on your work attire can potentially adversely impact your career. In my experience, management and others are paying attention to your appearance, and the way you dress can significantly impact your chances of getting that next promotion.

Inappropriate attire can also cause others not to take you seriously. When giving a presentation or chairing a meeting, you want your colleagues and clients to focus on your message and not be distracted by your anatomy, makeup, jewelry or fragrance.

Be mindful of fragrances. You don't want your fragrance walking in before you, permeating the atmosphere, or leaving a trail when you walk away. Many people are allergic to fragrances and will not readily express their discomfort. Make sure your fragrance is mild and that you keep it to a minimum. You do not want people avoiding you because they are adversely affected by your fragrance.

How should you dress? How do you know what is appropriate attire? Dressing conservatively is usually your safest bet. However, if you are new to your work environment and you are not sure how to dress, take a close look at the successful people in your organization. How are they dressed?

You do not have to spend a lot of money; you just need to make sure that you start off with two professional suits and other accessories that you can mix and match. Then, build your wardrobe over time.

If you look and behave like a highly trained and well-groomed professional, you will give yourself that competitive edge that can potentially increase your chances when competing for that next promotion. You are also more likely to earn the respect of senior management and your peers.

Will dressing professionally get you a promotion or ensure a successful career? Absolutely not, but what it will do is give you a competitive edge and a priceless first impression. Everything being equal between you and another candidate, the choice may just be you.

How are you going to differentiate yourself? What is going to be your professional brand? What do you want your legacy to be?

> *"Be who you are and say what you feel,*
> *because those who mind don't matter*
> *and those who matter don't mind."*—Dr. Seuss

5. Improve Your Communication Skills

Your career survival and competitiveness can depend on your ability to communicate effectively. Everyone from the CEO to first-line supervisors must be able to inform, persuade, and motivate diverse groups effectively. Make it a priority to find your voice early in your career.

Two of the most valuable skills to develop for a successful career are your verbal and written communication abilities. The higher you move up in the corporation, the more important it will become that you are able to address senior management, present ideas, and represent your company at industry functions.

Excellent communication skills are priceless as you negotiate on your own behalf or when representing your company. An effective communicator has the power of persuasion and can influence and guide the decision-maker. It will give you the ability to exchange thoughts effectively and clearly convey ideas when trying to reach a consensus or a mutually acceptable solution.

The value of excellent communication skills cannot be underestimated as they are necessary in all walks of life. Effective communication is a fundamental skill that all leaders or aspiring leaders should possess. Leaders are constantly requested to present the company's views on a public issue or its own mission, vision, and values. Leaders must also be able to communicate strategy, guidance, and direction to their employees. Ineffective communication leads to confusion, poor decisions, and a lack of leadership.

Addressing an audience whether it is your peers, management, or delivering a speech in public takes practice, and the more you practice, the sooner you will be able to develop a style that works for you early in your career. The more you practice, the faster you will understand your strengths and weaknesses. So accept as many speaking engagements as you can. The more you practice with internal presentations or delivering speeches to external audiences the faster you can refine your speaking style. Practice builds experience and confidence, which are the keys to effective speaking.

You can also take a speaking course, preferably one that videotapes your progress, so that you can learn how to present with confidence and conviction. A course can help you gain confidence in presenting your material, overcome nervousness and inhibitions, and help you formulate your thoughts when under pressure.

Consider joining Toastmaster. Toastmaster is an international organization that helps people overcome the fear of public speaking. Toastmaster is especially suitable for people that are shy or lack confidence. Toastmaster chapters are all over the world. You can find a local group on their website.

Feeling some nervousness and apprehension before giving a speech is natural and can be beneficial, as it keeps you alert, focused, and aware of your surroundings and audience. However, too much nervousness can be detrimental and cause you to draw a blank on portions of the message you intend to deliver. If you falter do not apologize, as this will only draw attention to your mistake. Chances are no one noticed. Most people are not active listeners and most likely will not remember 100% of what they heard. Also, keep in mind that your audience does not want you to fail; they want you to succeed because they want to be informed, stimulated, and entertained by your speech.

When I have to deliver a speech, regardless of the length, I first identify my audience and the key message I want to deliver. I make sure that I am well-versed in the material I'm about to deliver by writing it down, as this helps me to remember all of the major points. I either practice out loud or rehearse the speech in my mind. Practicing helps me with the flow and ensures that I stay within the time limit. If possible, I like to get a feel for the room and equipment. For example, I have discovered that I do not feel comfortable with a handheld microphone; I prefer a lavaliere or lectern with a microphone attached. These little preferences can make an enormous difference in your comfort and ease while delivering your message. Discover your preferences as soon as you can. Developing your speaking style and preferences will be a priceless skill to possess as you progress your career.

While the value of outstanding verbal communication skills cannot be diminished, you cannot minimize or ignore the value of written communication skills, as they are equally essential for effective communication.

Writing well is a skill that can be learned, developed, and nourished; however, this process takes time, patience, practice, and focus. You have to give yourself sufficient time to think through and develop your topic, whether you are writing internal memos, corresponding with clients, or writing a technical position paper.

Getting started is the hardest part, so start at the beginning, middle or end of your message. Start putting thoughts on paper, capturing whatever comes to your mind on the topic without concerning yourself about typos, verb tenses, or flow. If it helps, develop an outline to help organize your thoughts. When you have run out of thoughts, go to the beginning and read what you have written. In the process, you will find yourself editing, deleting, and expanding on ideas. Do this a number of times until you have fully developed your thoughts. Then go back and "unclutter" your document, removing redundancies, qualifiers, or other words and thoughts that do not add value or support your message. As a final step, make sure you carefully proofread your document. Depending on the importance of your document, you may want to have someone else read it. You will be amazed at what a fresh pair of eyes will pick up. If you have the luxury of time, put the document away for a day or so and then review with a fresh mind.

In today's environment, with most people opting to write e-mails, text messages, or instant messages, it is vital to be able to get your point across in a few lines. So your communication must be crisp, clear, concise, and effective. Many people are lazy about reading and may ignore your message if it is too long or drawn out.

The better your writing skills are, the better the impression you will be able to make. You never know exactly where your written communication will end up and who will read it and make a judgment about you. You can never take the quality of a written document for granted, because it takes on a life of its own after you send it. You never know how it will be used or how far a favorable impression might take you. Take the time to identify your targeted audience and the message you want to convey in a concise and professional manner.

One caution on written communication is to beware of the poison-pen syndrome. In today's environment, where people are reluctant to picking up the phone or walking down the hall, most of our communication is in writing. As such, we must be extremely cautious of how we respond and what we commit to writing.

Do not respond to an e-mail when you are still angry and reacting to someone else's hostility. This type of response on your part can be lethal for your career. It may feel good to get it off of your chest, but I guarantee that you will most certainly regret writing it when your own words come back to haunt you. Leaving written evidence that puts you in an unfavorable light can wreak irreparable damage on your career.

Sending angry or derisive memos, e-mails, or text messages might make you feel better for the moment, but they can seriously damage your credibility and career. Your words can and will be used against you. Your boss or human resources department may not be privy to the entire story when they are viewing your derogatory message.

Instead, use the poison pen to write your initial draft and get it off your chest, but do not send it. Sleep on it, and then come back to it when you have cooled off. You will be amazed at how your perspective can change overnight. Do yourself and your career a favor: stop, think, and reflect before you write and send a message.

Finally, just like verbal skills, practice, practice, and then practice some more. The more you do it, the easier it gets, and the benefits you will derive from excellent communication skills are priceless.

Work on developing your verbal and written communication skills early in your career. Ineffective communication leads to confusion, poor decisions, lack of leadership and can have an adverse impact on your career progression.

> *"Communication—the human connection—is the key to personal and career success."—Paul J. Meyer*

6. Establish Yourself as a Leader

Leadership is not defined by your job title, and it is certainly not limited to your boss or senior management. You do not have to wait to be assigned a supervisory or managerial position to practice and develop your leadership style. Leadership skills are developed over time with practice and experience. If you aspire to have a formal leadership position within your organization, you should start developing, refining, and defining your leadership style immediately.

If you are currently in an individual contributor position, meaning that you do not have a staff reporting to you, look for opportunities within your day-to-day activities to develop and exhibit your leadership skills. There are numerous ways in which you can develop and hone your leadership skills without a formal title.

- Establish yourself as a leader by demonstrating you are a dependable problem-solver, a great resource, and always a team player who is willing to offer solutions to problems and invest the required time and effort to ensure that things get done. For example, if you identify a problem within your working environment, go to your boss and advise him of the issue, provide a solution to the problem, or identify an opportunity that can be capitalized on as a result of your findings.

- Seize any opportunity to lead a work team as it is the perfect venue for showcasing and honing your leadership skills. If an initiative requires leading a team, listen to your team members and colleagues. Lead brainstorming sessions with your team to ensure that everyone is heard. These sessions may generate an innovative idea that will make you look like a hero, and your team members will appreciate your inclusive behavior, appreciate being heard, and most importantly, believe in your ability to lead. As the team leader, you are responsible for the outcome of the initiative. If things don't work out, you will be responsible for delivering the message to your management. If things work out well, you will get the credit. In this case, I encourage you to make sure that you recognize and give credit to the rest of the team. After all, you did not accomplish the results by yourself, it was a team effort.

- Volunteer to head internal groups or events. Are there any social or employee resource groups in your work environment? If so, run for office; this is an excellent opportunity to develop your leadership skills in a safe, low risk setting and environment. For example, I served as vice president and then president of our Latino organization, representing our Latino employees within the company. I also represented our company at numerous external events hosted by our organization's foundation. This option will help you develop and refine your leadership, communication, and networking skills as you host both internal and external events.

- Find your voice. Develop and perfect your speaking style by accepting as many speaking engagements as you can. Leaders or aspiring leaders should possess the ability to speak in public and address their employees. As a leader, you will be required to communicate strategy, guidance, and direction to your employees or represent your company at industry functions.
- Mentor another employee that can benefit from your experience. Serving as a mentor is an excellent way to improve your leadership skills and can also be extremely rewarding. Mentoring can be mutually beneficial as you can bring out the best in others and help them reach their highest potential while increasing your effectiveness as a leader. My most rewarding role was serving as mentor to the young employees in our company, to help guide them through the corporate maze in the early years of their careers.
- Have someone mentor you. A mentor can coach you on actions you can take to help you develop your leadership skills and how to be an effective supervisor.
- There are numerous websites and books on leadership. Surf the web or go to your local bookstore and browse until you find a book or program that meets your needs and start developing your leadership style.

A leader has multiple attributes that distinguish him from his peers, that his co-workers can look up to and that management can depend on to lead a project, initiative, or department. Do not be afraid of the challenges and responsibilities that come with being a leader.

You should strive to emulate some of the personal qualities possessed by all great leaders: *honesty, integrity, commitment to high standards, self-confidence, flexibility, and interpersonal skills.*

It is never too early to start honing your leadership skills. When developing your leadership style, remember that an effective leader inspires and influences others by example, helping others within a positive environment to reach their fullest potential.

"A good leader inspires people to have confidence in the leader; a great leader inspires people to have confidence in themselves."—Eleanor Roosevelt

7. Get off the Fence

Decisiveness is an essential aspect of getting ahead. Decisive people are respected and tend to get promoted. They stay cool and calm under pressure. They take charge during a crisis and usually have a plan which they execute with purpose and direction.

The indecisive person, on the other hand, is excruciatingly and painfully slow to make a decision. As a result, they make little to no progress in their careers. These people tend to get stuck, petrified by the thought of having to make a decision. In the meantime, opportunities pass them by, and they never seem to move toward their goals. The thought that making one decision could potentially close the door to an opportunity petrifies them.

Some crucial decisions can be frightening to make, but in some cases, not making a decision can cause you to lose a unique opportunity that may not be available at a later time. You should strive to seize the opportunity when it is presented to you.

From time to time, we have all struggled with making a certain decision. However, for some people it is a bit more complicated, because they like to please everyone. They don't want to make waves or let anyone down, which leads to indecision for fear of hurting others. Some tend to over-analyze and become paralyzed by their own analysis.

However, just making decisions is not sufficient, as bad or hasty decisions can cost you your career. You need to be decisive and also have the ability to weigh and balance your options, so that you ultimately make a decision based on the best information available to you at the time.

Think about past decisions. Is this situation similar to a past decision? In that case, what did you learn from that last decision? It's often been said that those who don't understand history are doomed to repeat it. Sometimes we make the same poor decisions over and over again.

You don't always have the luxury of time to sit down and analyze a situation, and it is, therefore, harder to make the right choice under pressure. In those situations, go with your intuition, your gut feelings. Several scientific studies have shown that a correct gut feeling can hit us before our brains can even rationally process what is going on. Think of the numerous times you ignored your gut feelings just to have them confirmed at a later time.

While listening to your gut seems straightforward, most people tend to ignore these feelings. Unfortunately, intuition doesn't always seem rational, and you may think you are overreacting or making too much of something because it rarely spells things out, giving instructions that you can clearly understand.

We are constantly being bombarded with intuitive messages in different forms. Sometimes it's a gut feeling when you know that something is not right or that something is about to happen, but you do not have any evidence to substantiate or define the feeling. Sometimes it can be an overwhelming feeling that you should be elsewhere, doing something or avoiding a certain place or thing. Or it can be a fight-or-flight response that causes those little hairs on the back of your neck to stand up, to warn you that something bad is about to happen.

In all cases, the messages aren't always as clear as we would like them to be or as easy to understand, which is probably why many people do not follow their intuition. Even though the messages aren't always clear, they can sometimes be repetitive, and that is when you need to pay attention to your intuition.

Learning to empower yourself by taking the driver's seat in the decision-making process will go a long way. So weigh the pros and cons of each option and consider the absolute worst thing that could happen and whether you could live with that worst-case scenario. If possible, "try on" your decision, wear it for a day, and see how it feels. Then let those feelings either guide you toward that option or steer you away.

Finally, if you still can't decide, and everything being equal with your options, toss a coin. Pay attention to your feelings. Are you secretly hoping for one outcome or the other? Are you disappointed or elated with the outcome of the toss? Your feelings can be an indicator of which option you should choose.

There are numerous websites that provide help and guidance for making efficient and effective decisions. Surf the web or your bookstore and browse until you find a book, article, or program that resonates with you and your gut feelings.

Decisions are at the heart of success, and at times there are critical moments when they can be difficult, perplexing, and nerve-wracking. However, always keep in mind that your view of a situation is governed by your perceptions and assumptions. So when faced with difficult choices, evaluate, investigate, and make an informed decision.

Decisiveness is one of the key ingredients to a successful career.

"It doesn't matter which side of the fence you get off on sometimes. What matters most is getting off. You cannot make progress without making decisions."
—Jim Rohn

"When making a decision of minor importance, I have always found it advantageous to consider all the pros and cons. In vital matters, however, such as the choice of a mate or a profession, the decision should come from the unconscious, from somewhere within ourselves. In the important decisions of personal life, we should be governed, I think, by the deep inner needs of our nature."
—Sigmund Freud

8. Find a Mentor

We all need mentors along the way. No matter the stage of your career, a little mentoring along the way is always a smart idea. Think of it as stopping to ask for directions when on a road trip. There is no way I could have accomplished everything I did without the help and support of others.

You will often need someone to help you navigate your work environment and point out the land mines. These should be people that you know honestly believe in you and your abilities; and will be willing to help you navigate some of the challenges you may encounter in the workplace.

Mentoring offers an opportunity to establish an informal one-on-one environment for coaching and feedback. It gives you the opportunity to share and leverage experiences and maximizes your potential. It offers an excellent, reliable sounding board, an opportunity to learn from others' mistakes and successes. Mentoring gives you access to someone whom you can trust and who will be available to coach you through difficult times. Hopefully it will be someone with whom you can develop a long-term relationship.

Mentoring is an excellent way to get the lay of the land and receive good third-party advice on skills development and interpersonal relationships. Having a mentor, formal or informal, is like having access to a personal trainer. It gives you access to someone who can help you build exceptional skills. This personal career trainer is at your disposal, absolutely free, and everybody benefits. If it is a formal mentoring relationship, whether one day per month or one hour per week, for that hour or day it is all about you.

How do you establish a mentoring relationship? If your company offers a mentoring program, you have the opportunity to participate in a structured program. If not, you can develop an informal relationship with a colleague, or you can identify a senior manager or senior employee that you believe can help you achieve your goals.

A structured, formal mentoring program partners mentors and protégés with the goal of matching less experienced workers with seasoned employees for career development, guidance, and support. One of the primary goals of the program is to keep the protégé on track by providing the skills they need to reach their personal career goals. This structure allows an organization to offer its employees a valuable tool that can assist them in achieving their individual goals.

A structured program is ideal for the person that is shy. It is for the person that finds the task of approaching someone they do not know uncomfortable. This program eliminates the need for the protégé to make the first move.

An informal mentoring relationship, on the other hand, can develop naturally with a boss or colleague, takes place in every organization and is highly effective. The knowledge transfer that results from an informal relationship is extremely beneficial for both the mentor and protégé.

An informal mentoring relationship can also be established by identifying someone that you respect or someone that may have pursued a career path that you may have an interest in exploring. Most people are usually flattered when asked to be a mentor and if they have the time and ability will readily agree to do so. Once you have identified a potential mentor, schedule a meeting or lunch to discuss a potential mentoring relationship. During this conversation establish the following:

- Your career goals and how you believe this mentoring relationship will help you achieve your goals.
- Your expectation of the mentoring relationship.
- Why you chose him/her as a mentor. Give specific feedback on their strengths and characteristics which led you to believe they could help you reach your career goals.
- Do not assume that the person is in a position to mentor. Ask the person if they have the time and the ability to help you achieve your goals. If the person does not have the time, ask if they feel comfortable recommending someone else to coach and counsel you.
- Establish the type of relationship (formal or informal), timing, and frequency of meetings.

If you choose a formal mentoring program, try to commit to the program for at least one hour per month for one year. The relationship should not be prescriptive. You should tailor the amount of time to your specific needs. But, if the relationship is not working or the chemistry is just not there, do not be shy about expressing your feelings. After all, the relationship should be about your self-development and benefit, and you have to feel comfortable with your mentor. Likewise, your mentor has to feel that he or she has the skills, abilities, and time to help you.

For mentoring to work best, the mentor and protégé should establish a completely open relationship and a safe haven to share experiences and talk openly about strengths and weakness. Topics can include corporate values, reward and recognition, setting goals, your upcoming performance review, or specific projects. There are no limits to what you can discuss.

Do not limit yourself to just one mentor or one gender. There will be times when you will need advice from a male, and other times it will be a female. So try to find a successful male and female to mentor you. These should be people you know believe in you and your abilities. People that will be willing to help you navigate some of the challenges you may encounter in the corporate environment.

"People seldom improve when they have no other model but themselves to copy."—Oliver Goldsmith

9. Networking

If you are serious about your career, you have to learn how to network. You have to get out there and meet people in your work group, as well as people outside of your work group, department, or business line. You need to meet and interact with as many people as you can. These people may have networks of their own that you can tap into to help you reach your career goals. Get to know people, so people can get to know you. Networking takes time and effort, but it is well worth the benefits you may derive.

Networking helps you work smarter, not harder. Working hard and spending time with your head down will help you focus on your work; and most likely produce an exceptional work product. However, you should not be working so hard that you fail to notice the day-to-day developments in your work environment. Unfortunately, working hard and doing your job well doesn't always guarantee that your efforts will be recognized and rewarded.

Keeping your head buried in your paperwork will not necessarily equal a promotion or career success. What can make a difference in your career is networking with your peers, supervisors, their supervisors, and senior managers in your department and others throughout the company. This is not to imply that you can be lax about the quality of your work. This means that you need to add networking to your 'to do' list. You need to produce an exceptional work product, make your boss look good, and make time to network.

Networking is a skill like any other and the more you do it the better you become. It is about building professional relationships, contacts, and having those contacts know you. These relationships can help you discover how to achieve your career goals, make career decisions, and help you develop a network. Broadening your network can help you obtain the knowledge that may lead you to opportunities that may not be widely announced to other employees.

Most networking begins through casual everyday meetings and conversations on an elevator, coffee line, professional conferences, or informal relationships with your colleagues, to name a few. However, many people find it difficult or do not feel comfortable with going up to a person, introducing themselves, and making small talk.

What is small talk and how does it help? Small talk fills the voids in conversations, helps ease tense moments, sets others at ease, and helps us become acquainted with people we do not know. There are two ways to make initiating small talk a little easier.

The first way is to be well-informed and able to discuss general topics, which can include, but are not limited to, weather, news events, famous people, fitness crazes, travel, or sports. Develop and prepare your icebreaker, small talk opener. This should be something you feel comfortable saying and briefly discussing.

The second way to ease into small talk is by asking others about themselves, their family, work, or hobby without getting personal. When making small talk, try to avoid any political or religious topics which you feel passionate about, as your view may be offensive to a person that does not share your opinion.

You can practice striking up a conversation with the people you meet in your day-to-day activities and normal routine. The more you practice making small talk, the more comfortable you will become. So practice, practice, and then practice some more.

Some networking tips to keep in mind:

- When networking, you have to be somewhat of a politician. Outliers tend to get labeled as too radical. The safest way to go is not to be too controversial and complaining. Being too honest, blunt, or judgmental can hold you back or derail your career. At times, some things are better left unsaid.

- Get to know and care for as many people as you can, even those who can't help progress your career. If you make others feel valued, important, and appreciated, chances are that these people will support you and your initiative sometime down the road. Learning to work well with and respect everyone is the best practice.

- If you are not comfortable with outright networking, volunteer or join a social group at work. Oftentimes these groups are supported by senior management, and this will give you access to mingle with other successful professionals in a more structured setting. It is an excellent venue to meet people outside of your department and business line.

- Consider joining Toastmaster. Members of Toastmaster receive constructive evaluations and advice on networking and can help you build the confidence you need to network effectively.

- Invite a potential mentor or a colleague that you would like to get to know better professionally to lunch. The relationships forged during a breakfast, lunch, or dinner meeting can be extremely fruitful and beneficial for your career development. Start with some small talk to break the ice. Small talk will give you and your colleague the opportunity to get to know each other on a personal and professional level. Be respectful and remember that each encounter is an opportunity to learn and expand your network.

By socializing with your peers and supervisors, you build trust and can often be privy to privileged information that can help you position yourself for a career-enhancing opportunity.

"It isn't just what you know, and it isn't just who you know. It's actually who you know, who knows you, and what you do for a living."—Bob Burg

10. Project Confidence

Self-confidence is one of the key ingredients required for a successful career. Projecting a lack of confidence and knowledge will construct barriers that may impede the growth of your career. You need to project confidence and never think that you are not as good as or as smart as the people around you because of your cultural background or education. Have faith in your skills and abilities and do not allow the cultural mantra of the organization or your peers affect your self-confidence.

Some people appear to be born with self-confidence, but most have to work at it. Self-confidence can be developed and nourished. However, getting it right is a matter of striking a perfect balance between low-confidence and over-confidence that is realistic and represents your true ability.

Self-confident individuals:

- do not waste too much time worrying about what others may think and instead focus on the task at hand
- feel comfortable with themselves, their abilities, strengths, and weaknesses
- are willing to take risks, readily admit their mistakes and learn from them
- graciously accept compliments recognizing a job well done without downplaying or exaggerating their role in the situation
- know how to set and attain reasonable goals
- take the time to appreciate and celebrate their success

When I was given the opportunity to work in the Supply and Trading group, I was elated. These jobs were reserved for the MBA graduates from the top business schools in the United States, high flyers on overseas assignments, and others who had been in the industry for many years. This group was extremely competitive with a 'sink-or-swim' and 'every-man-for-himself' attitude. This assignment was a significant test of my abilities.

My elation did not last terribly long as I immediately started comparing myself to those around me; feeling less confident about my abilities to do the job and compete with others. My cultural background coupled with the fact that I had not completed my MBA made me believe that I was not good enough. I felt inadequate with only three years of part-time graduate work from Pace University around the MBA graduates from Wharton, Duke, Harvard, and Cornell. I let the people around me, and their credentials, affect my self-esteem and confidence in my ability to engage.

At that time, I talked myself out of greatness by feeling that I wasn't good enough and that no one would want to hear what I had to say. Fortunately, my lack of confidence did not last too long as I started seeing some of these same Ivy League MBA graduates unable to survive in the tough, competitive trading-room environment. Some did not have the killer instinct required to survive that dog-eat-dog environment. They had Wharton, Duke, Harvard, and Cornell; and I had Pace University, ten years of experience in the industry, and all of the lessons I had learned from my life experiences which had heightened my intuition and survival skills.

I guess it is human nature to experience an occasional secret fear that one is not good enough. You may feel that everyone else has it all together and that you are the only one struggling to keep it together. Don't let a false sense of self and the opinion of others affect your self-worth and self-esteem.

You can look up to people, but only if it is not at the expense of your own self-worth and self-esteem. Regard these people as your role models, people you want to learn from and emulate. And, as you grow in knowledge, strength, and status, stand beside them as your peers.

Management's beliefs and cultural mantra can create an environment of greatness, productivity, and exceptional performers. However, in order to fan the flames of greatness, management must expect the best from their employees, and they will be amazed at the results.

If management offers encouragement, opportunity, and the tools required, it is likely that the employees will step up with confidence and deliver. At the end of the day, most people want to excel, but some have just not been given the opportunity to showcase their talent.

Instead of focusing on faults, weaknesses, and education or lack thereof, management should be focusing on boosting their employees' confidence, greatness, and potential, and employees will develop into what their management perceives, encourages, and nurtures.

When we hire people into the organization, it is because we see something remarkable in them; then after the wooing is over, we forget about the unique qualities that attracted us to hire these individuals, and we fail to develop them.

All employees should have the opportunity to be fully developed to their full potential, regardless of their educational, social, or cultural background. If an employee is good enough to hire into the company, then he or she should be good enough to develop to their fullest potential. If you do not, you will never know if there is a genius in your midst.

Most corporations tend to label employees at the beginning of their careers without looking deeper into the person's true potential. As such, they tend to overlook the extraordinary skills and potential some people possess, rarely giving assignments that will showcase their true potential. You'd be surprised what some people can and will accomplish when given the opportunity to do so.

Be presumptuous enough to believe that you are just as good as, as smart as, or better than those around you and that you have a significant contribution to make.

Don't talk yourself out of greatness. Lord knows that there are probably plenty of people around you who are already working on that.

"Nobody can make you feel inferior without your consent."—Eleanor Roosevelt

"Believe in yourself and all that you are. Know that there is something inside you greater than any obstacle."
—Christian D. Larson

Chapter 5

Career Failure

It is often difficult to pinpoint the exact moment when your career derailed. The deterioration of your career could have been a gradual decline.

Your over-confidence or arrogance could have made you careless about details. Were you too arrogant and obnoxious and the law of cause and effect caught up with you? The law of cause and effect is the law of perfect balance, of logical sequence, and of inevitable consequence. Whatever a man sows, he must reap. After all, life is a zero-sum game, and life experiences must be in perfect balance.

Or it could have happened in one split second, when somebody above you needed a scapegoat, and you were it.

Sometimes careers fall apart because life is directing you to move in a different direction.

You did not make it to your current position overnight; it happened over time, with a lot of hard work, late nights, and dedication. Chances are your career derailed the same way, over time, one incident at a time.

Regardless of the circumstances, the deterioration of your career can be painful to experience. As you see your life at work falling apart, it soon starts affecting your personal life. Careers are meant to grow, expand, and flourish, not deteriorate and plummet.

Career failure can be difficult to overcome, and few people are able to recover their careers after it has obliterated their ego and self-esteem. Career failure can be a brutally devastating blow that leaves you feeling completely spent and depressed. It is a personal attack on your psyche that cuts way deep down inside, attacking every fiber of your being and soul.

You go through many emotions as you try to figure out what just hit you. You feel afraid and lost, because you cannot seem to identify with that person who has just failed. Going through these emotions is natural, and in order to heal the situation, you must go through every stage of the grieving process, which often includes disbelief, fear, anger, blame, and shame.

The process is different for every person, and some move through these emotions quickly while others linger an inordinate amount of time on each emotion. You may move back and forth between a couple of the cycles and back to the beginning, with each iteration lasting less time as you begin to move more quickly through each cycle, until one day it is just a fleeting thought. The key is not to get stuck; to move on as quickly as possible. Lingering too long on these negative emotions can impede your progress.

After you are done with the grieving process and you are finally humbled into acceptance, you need to have the courage to face the hard truths of your career failure, pick yourself up, and rebuild a more meaningful career on a sturdy foundation. It will require you to resist the continual urge to ask and try to figure out why this has happened to you. It is human nature to want to know, investigate, and understand what led to the situation. However, you should not waste too much time trying to figure out why something has happened to you. Chances are you may never know the *why*. So, let it go and move on with your life.

Success can only be achieved when you give no voice or power to failure. If you want to move forward, you have to try to move through the grieving process as quickly as possible and stop wallowing in self-pity.

Whenever you feel trapped in fear or confusion, you are most likely responding to appearances, ego-based fears, and judging a book by its cover. Challenge yourself to dig deeper into the storyline of that book and find the lessons and gifts that may be hidden between the lines.

At times, failure is the catalyst that provides the kick in the butt or the wake-up call many of us require and offers a fabulous learning opportunity. No one likes to be labeled a failure; however, some of us need to hit rock bottom in order to learn some of the crucial lessons required to succeed.

Failure is not an accident; it is the result of actions, inactions, and reactions to your environment or situation. It has a definite purpose, structure, and sequence that is meant to take you to greater heights in your life. Take the time to understand your situation so that you can make a plan and take definite action to structure your next move.

Every situation opens a door of opportunity, if we are willing to stop long enough to assess the situation and walk through the open door. We have to stop blaming others for our limitations or failures and look to the one place where limitations and insecurities breed and can be transcended: in our own minds. Stop giving power to failure and start trusting your inner compass to map out the route to a successful journey.

So have you truly failed, or is life redirecting your efforts to a more meaningful experience? You need to stop long enough to reflect and capture the lessons that the experience has just delivered, so that you can turn it into success.

Become an advocate, for your skills, confidence, and strengths, and not your insecurities and limitations. As a result, you will be more confident and poised and will soar, inspiring others as you empower yourself for that amazing career you deserve.

We all need to borrow a page from Abraham Lincoln's life story. He was a man who knew how to pick himself up, never give up, and is one of the greatest examples of persistence. Abraham Lincoln, the sixteenth president, was defeated for Congress three times, defeated for Senate two times, and defeated for vice president in 1856 before he became president in 1860.

Thomas Edison experimented with thousands of different materials before discovering the filament for the light bulb. When asked how he felt about all of his failures, he denied that he had any failures. He indicated that he had learned thousands of ways how not to make a light bulb. He persevered to the end. Many times failure is the first step towards success.

You are not defined by your past; your past simply prepares you for future greatness.

"Success is the ability to go from failure to failure without losing your enthusiasm."
—Sir Winston Churchill

"Our greatest glory is not in never falling, but in rising every time we fall."—Confucius

My Career Hits a Roadblock

In 1997, I moved to another level within the organization when I was moved into the global aviation group as the Business Development Manager for Latin America. The learning curve was steep, but I was truly enjoying the creativity and autonomy this job offered. The aviation group was a new culture, mindset, lingo, and focus. It was like working for a totally different company.

Late 1999, Mobil merged with Exxon who had ample aviation representation in Latin America. As a result of the merger, my job was eliminated, and I went back to the Trading Room, as Senior Supply Analyst in the Global Crude group, to await my fate with the newly merged company.

I was back in the Trading Room, doing supply analysis, and things were not looking good for me. It appeared that there was no place for me to go, and I felt as though my career had taken a couple of steps backward. I had to do something to ensure that I did not fall through the cracks of the on-going transition from the old to the new organization.

I scheduled a meeting with the managers working on the transition team who knew me and my abilities. I explained the recent move from aviation to supply, detailed my work history emphasizing the two years I had spent as Business Development Manager, and expressed my interest to move into a business development position within the new organization. They made no promises but vowed to keep me in mind should something open up.

Post-merger, January 2000, I was fortunate to be placed in a business development job responsible for the Latin

American portfolio, the job I wanted. But you know what the adage says, "Be careful what you ask for because you just might get it."

At that time, I failed to recognize the risk of venturing into new territory within a new company with new managers. For those of us who took the risk, it meant starting our careers anew. These were people who did not know us at all; in effect, we had no history with the newly merged company.

Within nine months of starting the new job, I was re-assigned within the same business development group, from the Latin American portfolio to handle the U.S. portfolio. Maybe I made too much of that re-assignment, but to me, it was like being fired. I was devastated. Nothing like this had ever happened to me, and the worst part of that entire episode was that I never quite knew or understood the *why*.

It wasn't so much the reassignment. It was the way it was handled by our management. It was as if they were moving a piece of furniture from one side of the room to the other without stopping to take into consideration the impact on those involved in the shift. The entire situation was shrouded in secrecy with no explanations. The decision had been made; case closed.

I spent a lot of time trying to understand and figure out where management was coming from. As I went through the classic periods of denial, anger, and depression, I refused to believe that the actions were intentional or malicious. Fortunately, I was able to move through each of these iterations in a year before I finally accepted the reality of my situation.

While managing the Latin American portfolio, I was traveling approximately seventy percent of the time, with a grueling workload. That year was the hardest I had worked in my entire life. I'm not sure how long I could have kept up that routine without affecting my health. Transitioning the business from our affiliates to headquarters was intense. It meant understanding every single aspect of every deal being negotiated. Once I had completed all of the transitioning, the portfolio was handed to someone else, and I got zero credit for the grueling work and schedule of the previous nine months. I think I was entitled to be a little hostile.

From 1982 to 2000, I had made significant strides within the company. I had been promoted ten salary groups in eighteen years. I had broken down the barriers that prevented a secretary from moving up to the Contract Administration group, the barriers that existed between Contract Administration and Supply Operations, the barriers that existed between Supply Operations and Crude Oil Trading, and the ones between Trading and Business Development.

I had moved from one professional group to the next, excelling every step of the way. I had that rocket in my pocket. But little did I know that, sometime between 1999 and 2000, I had managed to drop that rocket somewhere over the Atlantic Ocean. My career went from fantastic to not looking too good to bad to worse, and as my grandson used to say, "the worstest."

I went from being a well-known, highly respected professional with a career to an employee whom no one knew with a good-paying job. In effect, the ladder had just been pulled out from under me. After eighteen years with the company and having made such significant strides, I had to start over. This was a new beginning. This was another turning point in my career. I was forty-three years old, and not the right time to be starting a career.

This was the job I wanted, but the management structure coupled with the stress of getting a new organization up and running were fertile ground for misinterpretations and frustrations for all. This was one of the most frustrating environments I've ever had to work in.

I consider myself to be a particularly strong person. But the management structure coupled with the growing pains of the merged company broke my spirit and my resolve. The domineering, paternalistic, and stifling management style were extremely hard to work with. It stifled my personal, professional, and career growth. I felt as if I were suffocating under the weight of the unnecessary pressure.

The one consolation was that it was not just me who felt this way about working within this structure. There was a general consensus; everyone in the group agreed that this management style stifled the creativity of the group with unnecessary stress and undue pressure. Morale was at an all-time low and pressure at an all-time high under this management structure.

On the flip side, I know that I did not make life easy for management as I challenged every misconception that was being attributed to me. This manager had formulated an opinion without knowing me as a person or as an employee. No matter what I tried, there was no getting through. Once her mind was made up, or she had formulated an opinion, that was it case closed. Right, wrong, or indifferent, my fate with the new company had been sealed. No amount of hard work and determination will help you get ahead if you do not have supportive management that believes in you and your abilities.

That year, I was ranked at the bottom of our group with no credit for the transitioning of the Latin American portfolio. At that time, I did not put this action into perspective. This job was in the products-distribution side of the business, which was totally new territory for me. I had spent the previous eighteen years working in the crude oil side of the industry and knew little about our company's distribution business. All of the other folks in the group had some finished products, terminal, or pipeline background. So in hindsight being ranked at the bottom that year was not unreasonable. However, at that time, I let my ego take it personal.

In the corporate environment, this type of experience is exceedingly difficult to overcome. For all intents and purposes, this was a new company, with new management evaluating my performance. There was nothing I could do or say to influence the outcome. In this person's eyes, my lack of distribution experience disqualified me to be a member of this elite group of people.

Things were so bad under this management structure that I finally decided that it was time for me to move on. I was forty-three years old, in a new company, under new management, and I did not stand a chance. The writing on the wall stated that my career was over. Was this the end of my journey? Is it possible to get back on track after your career derails? These were questions I had no answers to.

Even with those unanswered questions, one of the things, I had always vowed throughout the years was to recognize when I no longer had a career. This new company was offering a job, a well-paying job, but I did not want to kid myself into believing I had a career. I had to re-assess my aspirations of moving ahead, because upward mobility at my level was reserved for a limited few. These were large and competitive rank groups, and any misstep could be detrimental to your career obliterating any chance of promotion. The higher one goes up in the organization, the fewer the jobs and the tougher the competition.

So I embarked on a trip to the world of résumé-writing and job hunting, to try to find the answers to my questions. I worked on this process diligently for about a year, and nothing of substance materialized. I read all of the relevant articles; I consulted a professional career counselor and signed up with an executive search agency. There were a couple of offers, but none that matched my compensation and benefits package. I realized that, at my age and salary requirement, it would be extremely difficult to move to a new company. I had to face the reality of my situation and resign myself to the fact that I no longer had a career, and for reasons unknown to me, I was destined to remain with this company.

I spent one full year doubting my abilities and worthiness which was a complete waste of valuable time. Self-pity is a powerful, negative emotion that can hold you hostage and blackmail you emotionally. This mindset did nothing for my personal or professional growth. The intriguing part of this entire situation was that this reaction was totally out of character for me; I had never reacted in this manner before. This was the first time in my adult life that I let anyone break my spirit or let a situation define me as a person.

I felt as if someone had reached deep inside and tried to rip my soul out. But in reality, I was reacting to the devastation and obliteration of my ego and self-esteem, not to the person who was controlling my career or lack thereof.

I truly believe that nothing happens by accident or sheer coincidence. All of our relationships play a specific and pivotal role in molding who we are and who we will be in the future. I learned an extremely valuable lesson from my relationship with this manager. I vowed never to let anyone break my spirit and resolve.

I finally decided to stop fighting my situation and just go with the flow. After a year, I was finally humbled into acceptance, and decided to face the hard truths of my career failure. For some reason, destiny was keeping me in this job and this company. I decided to sit back, stop feeling sorry for myself, and see what destiny had in store for me.

I stopped long enough to reflect on all of my blessings and put my current situation into perspective. I had a lot to be thankful for, and all of the blessings outweighed this one devastating experience. I was certainly grateful for everything I had been able to accomplish and the fact that I had a great-paying job with excellent benefits, which was so much more than many could claim.

I decided to put all of the negative experiences behind me, where they belonged and where they should stay. I could not let this one experience define who I was as a person or my potential to move forward. So I decided to shift the power from the situation that was holding me hostage to viewing my career from an empowered position.

Once I was able to get off the road of self-pity and woe-is-me, I decided to go back to my own core values and change my attitude by simply asking what I could learn from this experience. I recognized that I had to change my attitude, because it is not productive to harbor two strong emotions at the same time. Each emotion will determine your mindset and next steps, and there is no way to go simultaneously in two different directions. There was no way I was going to move ahead while feeling like a complete failure.

In order to extract the lesson of what this situation offered, I had to step back and analyze the situation from an empowered vantage point. What did I contribute to this situation? At the time, I was too angry to resist the temptation to judge the person and to lash out at the situation with a knee-jerk reaction of hostility. I did not give the situation time to settle, develop, and reveal its true insight and message. I did not take time to understand the bigger picture. I judged the book by its cover, never digging deeper into the storyline and reading between the lines to extract the lesson the situation brought. I let my emotions drive my response, actions, and reactions.

If faced with this same situation today, I would put my ego and pride aside and not internalize or personalize the situation. I would resist the temptation to go into victim mode and become a hostage to my own hostility. I would instead try to get down to the *why* of the decision without wasting too much time rehashing the issue. After all, we shouldn't assume we always know why someone has done something or why a certain decision has been made.

People have their own reasons for doing things, and we can't always jump to the conclusion that it is about us in particular. Often the politics and bureaucracy of a large organization dictate certain actions that may be necessary due to information we are not and never will be privy to, and we simply become collateral damage. There may be a bigger issue that needs to be resolved and certain actions may be required to ensure its resolution. And the reality is that in many cases someone above you needed a scapegoat and you were it.

I decided to explore what I could learn from this difficult situation. This turned out to be the best strategy for me in coping with the turmoil and upset of my career. I took back control of my career by choosing to make this situation part of my informal education, and I emerged feeling both a sense of honor and responsibility to repair my reputation and career.

Once I changed my mindset and attitude, things started to change for me. It wasn't an ideal situation but, we had finally learned to respect and understand each other. There was never a formal apology, and I do not know for sure that one was warranted, but the fact that this manager acknowledged my strengths and abilities, and added that what had occurred early on was an "unfortunate situation", was good enough for me.

Today, I see this entire situation differently, because I truly believe that some higher power stepped in to redirect my life's journey.

Once I settled down long enough to dig into the storyline, it dawned on me that destiny had stepped in to change my path through this experience. For whatever reason, I was not meant to work in the Latin American region. Early in my career, there were two jobs available, one working with Nigeria and the other with Latin America. Despite my bilingual skills, I was assigned to the West Africa job. The Latin America Business Development Manager job only lasted nine months, just long enough to transition the business to headquarters.

Who knows what fate awaited me with the constant travels to Latin America. I can say that I did encounter a couple of disturbing situations when traveling to Latin America. For example, the energy industry as a whole is predominantly male dominated, and more so in Latin America where the entire culture is predominantly male dominated. When in negotiations, not once did I ever sit across the table from another woman. The only women I encountered were low level staff employees, secretaries, or cleaning ladies.

On the surface, gender roles and attitudes toward Latin women are clear and straightforward: A woman's place is in the home. It was apparent to me that many of the men I encountered did not feel comfortable with my role in representing a major U.S. corporation.

Because I'm of Latin descent, many of the men assumed that I knew and understood the Latin culture, and a woman's rightful place. They used my heritage as a license to be disrespectful and make inappropriate comments and sexual innuendos. I have to admit that at first I was not sure how to handle this behavior. I was not accustomed to being treated this way by my male colleagues in the United States. As a result, I let the comments go the first couple of times. After the third time of inappropriate comments, I realized that I had to put an end to this behavior.

During one of our afternoon meetings, my first agenda item was sexual harassment. I opened our meeting with, "Let's get the sexual harassment out of the way so we can have a productive meeting without having to stop for foolish comments, because I am sure that if I were not a Latina you would not dare behave this way for fear of reprisal." As I looked around the conference room table, waiting for someone to make the first comment, no one said a word. Everyone just kept looking down at their notes. Thankfully, that was the last time I had to deal with the harassments and innuendoes.

One other time, there was a senior person from a Latin American company speculating on how much money the company would pay for my release if I were to be kidnapped. At that time, kidnappings were prevalent in Latin America. For some reason, I did not think he was kidding. The entire encounter gave me chills and left me feeling very uncomfortable. I'm not sure what would have transpired had I continued traveling to that country.

So what at times may be perceived as unfair, a roadblock, or failure can actually be a blessing in disguise. It may be that this option is closed to you because you are meant to be doing something else or to keep you from harm. So, stop and look around for another open door, and as you walk through, you will understand why you were impeded. The roadblock will disappear, and you can joyfully explore the new path destiny has paved for you.

Unfortunately, my knee jerk reaction and my manager's uninformed assessment had done a lot of damage to my career. It would take a long time and effort to restore and repair the damage from the self-inflicted wounds and the initial unfavorable assessment and evaluation submitted by this manager. I must admit that this manager did try to make up for the "unfortunate situation" and help me by recommending an assignment on a project that had high visibility. I remember not trusting her motives and not even being grateful for the opportunity to showcase my talents. As it turned out, working on this project was the first step in the reparation of my reputation and career.

Nothing in life lasts forever, and in the fall of 2001, we received the fantastic news that happy days were here again. Our group was being restructured. This was the best Christmas present I could have ever wished for. I was no longer angry or hostile, but somehow I knew deep down that a restructuring of our group was probably the best thing that could happen to me. The entire group was happy and welcomed the new reporting structure. As a result of the restructuring, we were reporting directly to the senior manager of the group.

Working directly for the decision-maker of our group was a turning point in lifting the dark cloud that was hanging over me. The first thing I did was ask to have a few minutes of our new manager's time. I asked that he view this as a new start for me. I requested the opportunity to prove what I could bring to the table. It was an open and genuine dialogue, and I was glad that he was receptive.

A year later, during my first performance review, he was extremely complimentary. The words he used were, "I see a vast improvement in your performance." I was flattered but also taken aback. People do not change their performance overnight. The quality of my work had not changed. What had changed were my attitude and the fact that I was now working directly for him, without someone else filtering the feedback of my performance. Although I was tempted to comment, I bit my tongue and decided that it was best just to say, "Thank you," and move on.

The following year, during the second performance review, he was extremely complimentary and had nothing but glowing reports and feedback on my performance. His words touched me in a way that I could not have anticipated or describe. I was so touched that I had to excuse myself from the conversation, because I was getting too emotional. He could not understand why I was so emotional. All he said was, "But this is all good. I don't understand."

Once I was able to gather myself, I went back to finish our conversation and explained to him that I did not think I would see the day when I had finally regained my reputation with the company. At that time, I also took the opportunity to give him a high-level overview of what I had accomplished during the first nine months as the Latin America Business Development Manager, how I had gotten no credit for my accomplishments, and how his recognition on that day was a significant milestone for me. All he said was, "I had no idea."

There are pivotal moments in our lives where the action or words of a person have an immense impact on our lives. This was one of those moments for me. I felt that I had finally been able to recover from that severe blow that had shattered my ego and my self-esteem, and left me feeling helpless. I was no longer feeling lost, because now I recognized and could identify with the person he was evaluating. I had regained my sense of self and was no longer mourning the loss of my career. I knew that I could now start making plans and hoping for a better and brighter future with the new company.

October 7, 2003 was a new beginning for me. I had regained my confidence and emerged from that dark period a stronger and more confident person. I went through a metamorphosis during which I shed any insecurities and doubts in my abilities. I emerged feeling equal to everyone around me, even the Ivy League MBA graduates. I felt that I was contributing just as much, and in some cases, even more than some of the people around me.

So after three years, I was finally able to answer my own question. It is possible to get back on track after your career has derailed; it just takes some ingenuity, hard work, determination, time, and mentoring.

"Many of life's failures are people who had not realized how close they were to success when they gave up."—Thomas A Edison

CHAPTER 6

MANAGING CHANGE EFFECTIVELY

Managing change means effectively managing our perceptions and fears. Change is the natural circle of life that brings about progress. Even though we can intellectualize that change is inevitable, we fight to keep the status quo, we try to hang on to what is most familiar. Clinging to the way things used to be may give a person a sense of security, but growth and progress can only come when we embrace change and accept the new opportunities and possibilities that come with new beginnings.

We all experience and manage change in different ways with some reacting unpredictable and irrational. If the change is our idea, we tend to embrace it enthusiastically, excited about the possibilities. However, if change is imposed upon us, we tend to rebel and resist adapting to change.

We need to learn to embrace change as a normal part of our lives and stop fighting with ourselves and the establishment. Our reaction, attitude, and perception of the change will either hold us back or propel us to new heights.

When Mobil merged with Exxon, many of Exxon's senior management and employees moved into our headquarters building. To me, it felt as though we had sold our home with the opportunity to continue living in the guest room. We lost the master bedroom, master bath, and someone else was calling the shots. We no longer had any say in how, when, and where things were done. It was a strange feeling. It was a confusing and emotional time in all of our lives.

During the transition period what people feared the most was the unknown, the uncertainty of how things were going to be. There were many uncertainties about the organizational structure, the company's business strategy, operating practices, routines, roles, and responsibilities. Many employees were required to interview for their current positions. As a result, stress was at an all-time high and morale at an all-time low.

Many of the employees lost their sense of purpose, self-esteem, credibility, and security. If not managed correctly, these emotions can be difficult to overcome, since we tend to be our own worst enemy and unwittingly sabotage our progress with negative thoughts and ideas.

Similar to career failure, when the change involves a perceived personal loss, the process becomes much more complex and harder to overcome as you go through periods of denial, anger, depression, and finally acceptance. You may move back and forth between a couple of the cycles and back to the beginning, with each iteration lasting less time as you begin to move more quickly through each cycle, until finally you wake up one day and it is just a fleeting thought.

Everyone perceives change differently. Some react positively, with renewed energy and excitement, while others have a more pessimistic view and perceive the change as the beginning of the end for them. As a result, they tend to become stressed, overwhelmed, and sometimes bitter individuals.

Change does not have to be stressful, overwhelming, or confusing if you manage your perceptions and fears. The transition period from the old to the new is the time to figure out how you will fit into the new organization. This is the perfect time to revisit your life and career, and clearly delineate what you want and envision for yourself. This may require that you leave some of the old ways that no longer fit behind.

Stay alert and focus on how the work changes are being implemented. Some will be gradual while others will be immediate. Is the organization creating new jobs, is there an opportunity for a new position or even a promotion as a result of the reorganization? Do these organizational changes involve learning a new skill? If so, what can you do to prepare and position yourself for a new assignment or promotion? Anticipating changes in your work environment will help you plan ahead and identify any training or resource that will help you better assimilate into the new organization.

Review current work processes and determine whether they need to be enhanced, eliminated, or whether they will work well within the new work environment. Then, take the opportunity to review your findings and potential solutions with the management team letting them know which processes worked well, which were highly deficient, and which will no longer fit into the new organization.

View the change as an opportunity to make a fresh start and, if applicable, resolve old issues. This is a time when the new organization is being shaped and defined, so take the time to sit back and figure out if there is any way you can make this work in your favor—a new position or a promotion before the new way is solidified and implemented. Look around and see what the new situation may have to offer: a better boss, exciting new challenges, new contacts, and career opportunities. Get a feel for the new organization and how you will fit into the new plan.

For example, during the time of our company's transition, I took the time to figure out who the decision-makers were, decided where I wanted to be in the new organization, and promoted my skills and brand, making a case for why I was the best person for the job. Fortunately for me, the person offered the job I wanted turned it down, and as runner-up, I got the job. I do not believe this would have been the outcome if I had not taken the time to explore the new organization and taken the initiative to promote my experience, skills, and desires about where I wanted to work.

Change, whether planned or unplanned, imposed or self-imposed, wanted or not, is necessary for your growth. Refrain from making assumptions, jumping to conclusions, and taking the change personal before you have had the opportunity to weigh and assess all of the facts.

Take it one day at a time, and remember that it is your perception of change that affects your thoughts, feelings, actions, and reactions.

Stop to examine how you perceive the change, and determine whether you are helping or hurting yourself with your perceptions. Focus on letting go of what is familiar and comfortable by embracing new beginnings.

Stop rehashing where you came from and how things were, and start getting excited about where you want to go and how you are going to get there. If you perceive the change as an opportunity for a fresh start, a chance to change direction, you can travel through the transition highway with few or no problems at all.

It is beneficial to view change as necessary for your personal growth. Embrace change and align your words, thoughts, actions, and reactions with your goals, and don't be distracted by perceived obstacles. Bask in the wonderment of the possibilities and new territories you will explore and the unique opportunity to re-invent yourself.

It is essential to have patience with yourself and the process of transitioning from the old to the new. You have made monumental strides and gained a great deal of practical experience and wisdom. All of this learning took time and effort and culminated in the incredible person you are today. Capitalize on all of that experience and put it to work for you in positioning yourself within the new organization.

Just in case all else fails, fall back on the Serenity Prayer: *"God, grant me the serenity to accept the things I cannot change,* the courage to change the things I can, and the wisdom to know the difference."

"If you don't like something, change it. If you can't change it, change your attitude. Don't complain."
—Maya Angelou

"Change is inevitable, growth is intentional."
—Glenda Cloud

CHAPTER 7

FEMALE LEADERS—BALANCING POWER ISSUES

Many experts agree that the ideal leadership teams should consist of a balance of men and women with their differing traits, management styles, risk profile, and collaboration. They also agree that the female brain and creativity can positively impact the bottom line. Today, there are many more women in the corporate environment, and many men do not know how to handle their creativity and unique way of problem-solving.

University of California-Irvine professor emeritus Judy Rosener reports that brain scans prove that male and female brains operate differently. Rosener concluded that a company with a leadership team that consisted of male and female will outperform a company that relies on the leadership of a single sex. Rosener also concluded that women aren't better, but they bring to the table something that men don't have and that a company dominated by women would not necessarily outperform a company dominated by men. (Judy Rosener cited in "Women slowly gain on Corporate America" by Del Jones in *USA Today* January 2, 2009)

Sandra Witelson, a neuroscientist, is in agreement with the differences in male and female brains, stating, "There are clear differences in the brain between men and women, both in structure and chemistry, which includes hormones and neurotransmitters and what's connected to what." Some studies show that, as a result of brain "structure and wiring," men use only one side of the brain to process some problems, while women employ both sides (*Why Are There Differences in Gender Behavior? March 2010*).

Similar studies have concluded that there are differences in the brains of adult men and women. However, these differences are a result of life experiences and the manner in which boys and girls are treated while growing up. These studies imply that brains can change their structure and function in response to the environment. (*Why Are There Differences in Gender Behavior? March 2011*)

Other studies support the notion that biology and upbringing have a lot to do with the differences between the genders. That gender differences come from nature and nurture. These differences in the cultural roots of men and women are also the roots of a gentler style of leadership skills.

Some research indicates that women have a *transformational* leadership style and men tend to be more *transactional*. This means that most women who adopt the transformational style are not only interested in getting the deal done; they are also interested in a collaborative, relationship building approach.

- The *transformational* leadership approach focuses on reaching the goals of the team and effecting change by serving as a role model, inspiring, motivating, mentoring, and nurturing in a participative and collaborative environment. A transformational leader adheres to the rules and regulations of the organization but is more likely to entertain an "out of the box" solution to a problem.

- The *transactional* leadership approach depends on a system of rewards and punishments and emphasizes getting things done "by the book" staying within the boundaries and rules of the organization. This approach is commonly seen in large organizations, which tend to be bureaucratic in nature.

So, is it nature, nurture, or a combination of the two? The answer to which of these theories is correct is still being debated. However, as mothers, daughters, wives, aunts, and sisters, women are relationship-builders, collaborative in their approach and intuitive by nature. Because women wear so many different hats, they develop a variety of skills that enhance their management perspective and leadership styles, which makes them valuable members of any executive leadership team.

Unfortunately, women are still taking a back seat and not claiming their right to the driver's seat when it comes to their leadership style, and too often they struggle with the issue of power and control at work.

At home, many women are CEO, CFO (Chief Financial Officer), and Board member of their families. They successfully lead their families, church groups, plan numerous social and charity events, and succeed in many other leadership roles in the home and social fronts. As mothers and wives, they have had the opportunity to practice and perfect their leadership skills, which in many cases are transferable to the workplace.

Eleanor Roosevelt's observation that "a home requires all the tact and all the executive ability required in any business" has been supported by two surveys. *Wellesley College Center for Research on Women* and the *Center for Creative Leadership in Greensboro, North Carolina* conducted individual surveys of approximately one hundred twenty (sixty in each group) successful female managers. These surveys confirmed that parenting teaches transferable skills and that multiple life roles enhanced their professional leadership performance. The surveys also found that most of the participants who had children thought that being a mother had made them better executives and had been an excellent training ground for developing their leadership skills.

However, when it comes to displaying these same leadership qualities at work, many women are afraid of exerting their power and style. They are afraid of taking a leadership position feeling unsure of their ability to lead and the perception of their peers. Some women feel intimidated by the extroverts and bullies in their work environment. As a result, they tend to become invisible not speaking up or giving themselves credit for all of the experience they have gained over the years.

Granted, rearing a family, managing the day-to-day of running a home, or planning events is not exactly the same as leading a work group. However, many of the skills required to lead a staff, project, or work team are the same as those required when running a home and raising children. As CEO and CFO of their families, women manage and resolve issues that enhance their leadership skills and performance:

- deal with and mediate difficult, challenging situations with spouse, children, and in-laws
- multitask, delegate, and collaborate with the rest of the family
- organizational skills are a must—have to be extremely organized to make sure that everything is perfectly planned, so that all tasks are completed on a timely basis
- prepare and negotiate schedules with other parents, sitters, and numerous other day-to-day activities and appointments
- negotiate with contractors and oversee home-improvement and construction projects
- develop budgets for their family's day-to-day and future expenses
- teach their children about values and ethical behavior

The above is the tip of the iceberg on the activities that require leadership skills. There are hundreds of examples of tasks women perform on a daily basis that hone their leadership skills.

Every woman will develop a different combination of skills depending on their family structure. The bottom line is that these skills are transferable to the workplace. Stop and think about all of the skills you have developed and perfected over the years in your day-to-day activities as CEO, CFO, and Board member of your family. How can you transfer those same skills to your workplace with the same confidence and effectiveness?

As a culture, we are still condemning women who are too aggressive or assert their right to power, even though these are the precise traits associated with effective leaders. This negative connotation puts women in leadership positions in a double bind, as they are faced with the formidable task of balancing authority without being autocratic.

If a woman chooses to be assertive and forceful, she is perceived to be a "bitch." If she exhibits too much compassion, then she doesn't have what it takes to handle a powerful leadership position. Power can be a tough balancing act for some women, but the key is to be assertive without the fear of being labeled a "bitch".

The bottom line is that women need to learn how to be assertive and stand up for their right to take the driver's seat. They need to come out of the shadows and make themselves visible to their management and peers; exhibit their personal power and charisma by speaking up for themselves in a confident manner without compromising their values. It is, therefore, imperative that women fully develop their communication skills so that they can communicate in a direct, concise, and compelling fashion.

Women can confidently showcase their power by openly displaying their knowledge, skills, and being prepared when addressing management, peers, and competitors. This way they will be judged as individuals with exceptional ideas that can positively impact the organization.

The key is to learn how to exert power and leadership skills in a manner that helps others and enhances your self-esteem and self-worth. Try not to let your work environment intimidate you. Do not talk yourself out of greatness. You should believe in your strengths and abilities and cast out any and all doubt from your mind. Develop an authentic, personal style that you feel comfortable with so you can showcase your talents without feeling intimidated by your peers.

If women continue to take a back seat, they are never going to achieve gender parity in the corporate environment. Women have to learn to take charge of their careers and their rightful place in corporate America as this is the only way they will achieve the recognition they deserve.

CHAPTER 8

ARE WOMEN THEIR OWN WORST ENEMIES?

Women have come a long way in the last thirty years but continue to have a long way to go before they achieve gender parity. Many women continue to face obstacles and barriers that hinder their ability to climb the corporate ladder and achieve the recognition they deserve.

In some industries women still find themselves grappling with and bumping up against the proverbial glass ceiling that says, "You can advance just this far but no further." Unfortunately, no matter how hard some women have tried over the years, they have not been able to shatter and completely remove that glass ceiling. Those women who have broken through the glass ceiling were able to do so because they set high standards for themselves. Hillary Clinton was not able to "shatter that highest, hardest glass ceiling" but left it with ~66 million cracks in 2016.

There are certainly many more women in the energy industry today than when I started, in 1982, nevertheless later in my career I still found myself looking around the conference room table and, more often than not, I was still the only woman.

Corporate America has made significant strides; however, it will take more time for the environment to become more women-friendly. Because no matter how smart, talented, or successful a woman is, there is still the cultural difference that separates men and women.

Early in life we learn that there are innate physical differences between men and women and although both have many things in common, society has created the male and female classification which we use to classify both ourselves and others. Historically, the differences between men and women have been socially defined by the male perspective which assumed that men were superior.

It is essential that we recognize both the similarities and differences between men and women. As we strive for equality between the sexes, we must be careful not to lose the importance of our differences when trying to be politically correct. The reality is that men and women are equal and should be treated equally when it comes to rights and opportunities. However, men and women are different when it comes to the obvious physical attributes and the less obvious psychological. The psychological differences can influence our view of the world, and how we develop and nurture our personal and business relationships.

Women should be considered equal to men, yet also be valued for bringing a fresh perspective to the workplace. More importantly, women need to recognize how these differences affect decisions within their own environment and learn how to maximize and use their innate abilities.

Claiming that you are bumping up against the glass ceiling implies that the corporation is not supportive of advancing women, and this may or may not be the case. Before claiming that you are bumping up against the 'glass ceiling', you should first take a long, hard look at your circumstance. Evaluate your current situation and make an honest assessment about what may be hindering your progress. For example,

- Is it education or a specific skill that needs to be developed and perfected? Depending on the nature of the job, an MBA or other advanced degree may be required.
- Have you developed a network?
- Have you identified your brand and developed a marketing plan for that product called *You*?
- How are your communication skills?
- When was the last time you volunteered to lead a work team or other work related event?
- Have you developed a career plan outlining your goals and aspirations and how you will reach those goals?
- Stop, think, and reflect on what you can do to help progress your career.

Unfortunately, when it comes to competing in the corporate environment, women can at times be their own worst enemies. Their own actions and behaviors can be one of the primary reasons women fail to get ahead in the corporate environment. In some cases, women overtly display jealousy toward their successful peers. This inability to control their emotions and exhibit a professional demeanor can sometimes be career-limiting.

Women need to learn how to manage controversy and competition in a more professional manner. Some women often spend too much time gossiping, backstabbing, and displaying inappropriate dramatic behavior. This is not only unprofessional, but it detracts their ability to get ahead. Women need to learn how to compartmentalize and let go. Women need to stop taking work related disagreements personal. Ten years later, women will still bring up the same disagreement. Ladies, we need to learn how to let go.

So where do women learn these obnoxious behaviors? More importantly, what do men learn growing-up that women are not privy to? Is it their prevalence to participate in organized sports, where they are fierce competitors on the field and then socialize after the event? I don't know what the answer is, but it appears that, as women, we are picking up some of these reprehensible behaviors from the female role models in our lives.

I have witnessed men compete for assignments and disagree on issues at work and at the end of the discussion they go to lunch, play golf, and for the most part support each other. They either don't take it personal or have the ability to mask their true feelings. They tend to move on and develop long-lasting relationships, which in turn translates into developing that next male executive.

Early in my career I worked in a group that was primarily women from the top down. This group was drama central. This type of environment can be like a three-ring circus, with all of the drama, distractions, gossiping, backstabbing, and inappropriate dramatic vindictive behavior. For the most part, the behavior was unprofessional when it came to working with someone they did not like, with most often falling victim to their own inability to remain objective while at work.

Unfortunately, almost twenty-five years later, this same group was still primarily women and still facing the same issues and still carries a negative connotation of not being sufficiently professional. This type of behavior that is distinct in women can be distracting, and women caught up in this behavior allow the rivalries—real or perceived—to cloud their judgment.

If you find yourself in such an environment, do your best to separate yourself from the drama, and just do your job; it will pay off in the long run. The key is not to let yourself get distracted by the drama around you. Maintain diligence when it comes to your priorities. Stay focused on your goals and objectives. Separating yourself from the distractions of the daily drama may not make you popular with your peers, but it will be much better for your career.

These detestable behaviors do not work in our favor in the corporate world. In fact, they are at the top of the list of why some women do not get ahead in corporate America. If women want to move the needle that measures gender parity, they need to start behaving differently, so that they can be better role models and teach the young ladies in the pipeline how to be professional competitors, win, lose, or draw.

Having qualified people in top jobs—or any job, for that matter—should be the objective of any employer. However, female role models in leadership positions should focus on ensuring that the young women in the pipeline get the proper training, education, and empowerment that will permit them to be better positioned for that next promotion, regardless of the assignment.

When you look around, you see women choosing and succeeding in careers, in many different fields. So you would surmise that now that women are succeeding, they would have developed a solid support system to ensure that the pipeline of successful women continues to flow. And to some extent, they have, just as long as the woman they are supporting is not perceived as a threat. As women move up through the corporate ranks, they often leave behind peers who are not happy for them and instead exhibit jealousy, envy, or resentment. I have personally experienced the overt resentment towards me when management announced that I was being promoted. There were no congratulations forthcoming from the women in our group.

The corporate arena can be extremely competitive, a survival-of-the-fittest environment. More often than not, underneath the sweetness and words of encouragement, there is a shark lying in wait ready to rip you apart or set you up for failure. Unfortunately, it is extremely difficult to identify such a person, because they are extremely masterful at hiding their devious side. As a result, it can be difficult to prove their depths of deception to anyone else, especially senior management.

These women never exhibit their true colors in front of their bosses, and senior management is often duped by their so-called professionalism, poise, confidence, and intelligence. Sadly, some of these women are on a mission to destroy your hopes and dreams. This is not to imply that some men do not behave in this manner because they do. However, since men are in the majority of the executive ranks, they are less likely to see a female colleague as a threat.

The higher women move up in the corporation, the uglier the behavior and fiercer the competition. This behavior is likely fueled by the fact that there are fewer jobs at the top of the pyramid, and each wants to be the one to get that next promotion. Not only are they competing with other women, but they are also competing with their male counterparts.

A 2008 study, part of behavioral scientist Shannon L. Goodson's book, *The Psychology of Sales Call Reluctance,* compared approximately 11,500 professional females with approximately 16,700 males from around the world. The study concluded that women can at times be their own worst enemies when it comes to climbing the corporate ladder. This international study found that women are less likely to promote themselves and network than their male counterparts. "Women did not create the glass ceiling, the invisible barrier blamed for limiting their ability to earn what they're worth, but they help maintain it," Goodson wrote.

A portion of Goodson's research conducted primarily in the U.S. indicates that many female executives are not as supportive or as encouraging of female staff, and at times even sabotage the chances of other female workers seeking promotion. The study also found that these female executives tended to "take the ladder with them," once they reached the top. "This led many women in the study to actually prefer male managers to female managers, claiming men are more consistent and fair-minded than women," Goodson added.

Many women in senior management positions often refuse to get involved and help promote and support other women. It is sad that the women we should be looking up to as role models are the ones exhibiting the least professional and most obnoxious behavior. These women tend to abuse their power. They do not use their power in a manner that will help other women in the pipeline.

My thirty-four-year career was in a male dominated industry. During that time, some had admitted to me that they were afraid of some of women in the corporate environment. Not because they are powerful, smart, or successful, but because some women were too sensitive and at times were unable to control their emotions. They too had encountered that shark lying in wait to rip apart anyone that impedes their path to the top of the organization. So what happens? John decides that he will play it safe and take Joe instead of Jane under his wing for development and advancement.

Ladies be realistic about your personal situation. Are there really gender issues in your environment, or is there some skill set that you are lacking or some behavior pattern that requires modification?

Chapter 9

Balancing Career and Family

Gender issues are not only about the glass ceiling. They are also about the delicate balancing of work and personal lives. Fortunately, many companies recognize that taking care of family matters and raising children aren't just women's issues—they are family issues.

Many women are torn by having to choose between having a family and their careers and must earnestly answer the question: Am I prepared to make the sacrifices that are required in order to break through the glass ceiling? More often than not, the answer is a resounding, "No, my family comes first."

Responsibility to family, childcare in particular, is one of the primary reasons why women leave the workforce, and this makes it challenging to have critical mass when it comes to quantifying women in the professional work environment.

Some believe that choosing to pursue motherhood and a career sub-optimizes both and opt for one or the other. Some of the most successful women in our corporate environment have made a conscious decision not to have children and instead dedicate one hundred percent of their energy to their careers.

Choosing between work and family is a highly personal decision that takes many circumstances into consideration, and only you and your family can make the final decision. At the end of the day, you have to be happy with your choice as to whether you want to be a stay-at-home mom, be a working mom, or be childless and dedicate your life to your career.

It is a fact of life that many women do not have the luxury of choice. Today, women represent approximately fifty percent of the workforce and two-thirds of women in the workforce are the primary breadwinner or co-breadwinner of their families. The ten most common positions held by women are not highly paid jobs. The majority of women are still administrative assistants, nurses, teachers, first line supervisors, and receptionists.

There is absolutely nothing wrong with these professions, but what is wrong is that women who hold these positions are still making less than their white male counterpart's income and much less if they are African American or Latina.

I've often wondered why women are paid less money than men for the same job. I suspect that this may be attributed to the outdated cultural social model that puts the man at the head of the family. Wake up America, the family structure has changed dramatically since the 50's, when most women were housewives and those who worked were doing so in order to supplement the primary breadwinner's salary or have their own spending money.

There is no longer just one model for the traditional family. In some minority cultures, women outnumber men in being the primary breadwinner for their families. And yet, minority women are the ones paid the least for their work, which forces them to take on more than one job. African American women and Latinas are carrying the burden of having to raise a family on much less than the balance of the population.

Then there are those that don't have to, but choose to, be working mothers. Many women who choose to be working mothers do so for numerous reasons. They want to have their own money, continue to advance their careers, maintain their independence, or keep their identity, to name a few.

Regardless of the reason a woman opts to be a working mom, the guilt of leaving the children in the care of others is often a serious factor in her peace of mind. She often feels conflicted about where her schedule requires her to be versus where she would prefer to be. In fact, approximately fifty percent of working moms feel guilty at least once a day. The key for working mothers is to try to manage the feelings of guilt. Guilt is a negative emotion that can potentially hinder a working mom's ability to make effective and efficient decisions that can cause her to fail both at work and home.

It is difficult to concentrate on work if you do not have reliable childcare. A trustworthy and dependable childcare provider helps working parents financially and emotionally.

Knowing that you have a person that you can trust with your children without worrying about their well-being is priceless.

Having reliable daycare helped me accomplish my educational and career goals. I could not have done it without the help of my husband and the woman who became our sitter, grandmother, and mother for the seven years my children required care.

Fortunately, my husband was way ahead of his time by being the only Mr. Mom I knew at the time. During the early to mid '80s being a Mr. Mom was not common or popular, and taking care of children was considered a woman's job especially in the Latino community. He was willing to take on some of the duties in the home and the responsibility of the day-to-day caring of our family.

After work, my husband picked the oldest up but would leave the youngest with the sitter until I came home from school. With my husband's help, an excellent sitter, and Pace, a university that met the needs of working students, I was able to achieve my career and educational goals.

My husband and I had an equitable distribution of responsibilities in the home. For example, depending on our schedules, whoever came home first would make dinner, while the other picked up the boys from a sporting event. We capitalized on each other's strengths and expertise in dividing up the responsibilities in the home front.

The bottom line is that all of the responsibility for taking care of the children and home should not rest with the woman, especially if she is a working mother.

Whether you work full time or part time, finding the balance between your career and your family is crucial.

Many parents struggle to find the right balance between their careers and nurturing their relationship with their children.

There is no single solution to balancing both worlds. Each family's situation is as unique as each of its members. Your family's health, economic condition, extended family, and resources at your disposal as a parent will dictate the best solution for you. The key is to stay true to yourself, your goals, and your family.

While it is hard to break the glass ceiling, it's even harder when you are raising children. Women wear many more hats than men as caregivers, nurturer, and home keepers. As a result, women are required to take off more time from work than men to resolve family issues.

When women are formulating their plans on how best to balance their career and family, they should also include a balancing of duties in the home front. In many cases, there needs to be a more equitable distribution of duties between women and their significant others. This balancing of duties can go a long way in helping a woman succeed in her career and her family as a mother and wife.

Depending on the choices you make, you can certainly limit or even end your career. The fact of the matter is that someone has to be available to take care of the children and the home, whether it is the man or woman.

Young women in the workforce need to understand that they do not have to be stay-at-home moms in order to be excellent mothers. They can be excellent mothers and still have a successful career. It does not have to be one or the other. They can do both. It just takes a little more time management, organization, patience, and ingenuity.

The essential thing is to be true to yourself, with the goal of balancing and integrating both worlds successfully, if you choose. In doing so, remember to take care of yourself first. Too many women are so focused on taking care of family members and work responsibilities that they tend to forget about their own personal needs. The safety message on the airplane tells you to put your oxygen mask on first before helping the person seated next to you; this philosophy also applies on the ground.

CHAPTER 10

THE GLAMOROUS WORLD OF BUSINESS TRAVEL

Many people truly believe that business travel is glamorous, and maybe it was at one point in time. But the travel experience—whether for business or pleasure—has lost its appeal for many. Extensive travel grows old very quickly with reduced, delayed or canceled flights, crowded planes, reduced services offered by the airlines, bad meals or no meals on the flight, missing connections, endless waiting at airport lounges, and intense airport security; to name a few.

You are constantly surrounded by people, yet it can make for a lonely existence. Even the place you call home is no consolation, since you spend so much time away from there that you have the same problem in meeting people and developing relationships.

On the other hand, there are aspects of business travel that can still be appreciated. You get to take advantage of some of the small luxuries such as not making the bed, using a different towel every day without having to worry about piling up the laundry, enjoying a free meal and drink, which can translate into a more pleasant trip. You get to meet new people and visit places you would probably not make an effort (or could not afford) to visit.

In our global economy, travel is a fact of life, and for many business people, travel is a frequent event. I have had many different jobs that required both domestic and international travel. Two assignments required seventy percent travel. As a result, I have come up with ways to simplify being away from home and minimize getting stressed, overwhelmed, exhausted, and travel safely. Throughout my years of extensive travel, I have learned some travel tips that have made my travels easier. If you plan ahead, traveling can be less stressful.

- Whenever possible, use a carry-on bag to avoid having to check your bag or having your bag not reach its destination. This will save you time as you do not have to wait, in long lines, to check your bag, nor wait endlessly for your bag to travel from the plane to the arrivals terminal at your destination.
- If you do check your bag, make sure you pack a small carry-on with your essential toiletries, medications, and one change of clothes, just in case your bag does not make it to its destination.
- Keep a fully stocked packed toiletries bag, even if you don't know when or where your next business trip will be. A pre-packed toiletries bag may seem like a waste of money, to keep

duplicates stored away, but this step will save you valuable time and ensure that you have all of your essential products when you are away from home. The bag should contain a trial size of all or most of the products you use throughout the course of an average day, from deodorant to a toothbrush and everything in between.

- Most hotels provide personal items such as an iron, clothing steamer, hair dryer and basic toiletries. Once you get familiar with the amenities offered by most hotels, you can certainly minimize what you have to pack.

- Always check the weather and local news of your destination. This will help you plan your wardrobe and avoid getting surprised by canceled flights and grounded airplanes.

- When planning your wardrobe for your trip, try to stay away from linens and cotton, as they tend to wrinkle. Most hotels have irons and ironing boards, but who wants to have to iron clothes.

- When packing your bag, rolling instead of folding your clothes will not only minimize wrinkling but will also take up less space. Stuffing smaller items, such as undergarments, socks, and hoses, inside your shoes or in any open space between the rolls will also help maximize the use of the space in your bag. This will not only save space in your bag but will also keep your shoes from getting squashed.

- Don't pack more than you need. Try to stick to one color theme, to avoid having to pack multiple shoes or other accessories. One business suit with several different shirts can usually get you through a few days. For example, men can wear the same suit with different-colored shirts and ties and no one will notice. It is a bit more difficult for women; however, one skirt, one jacket, and a pair of slacks can be mixed and matched with several blouses or scarves.

- Develop a travel profile with your preferences. Determine where you like to sit when on an airplane, and request that specific area when making travel arrangements or checking in.

- If on international travel, make sure that you know the location of and have contact information for your home country's Embassy before you travel.

- Establish an emergency contact either with your company, the company you are meeting in the foreign country, or both.

- Always carry sufficient cash and make it a point to know what and how much needs to be paid when entering or departing from a foreign country. Today most places will accept debit or credit cards. However, it still does not hurt to be informed.

In 1998, I was leaving Quito Airport in Ecuador, and there was an exit tax that had to be paid to American Airlines. To my surprise, American Airlines would only accept cash payment. No matter how much I pled with the airline, they were not budging. I refused to take no for an answer and kept begging American Airlines to take my credit card payment, to no avail. After fifteen minutes of pleading with the airline, a kind music student traveling to the United States offered to pay the fee for me. I gratefully accepted and asked for her address in the States where I could send repayment. Unfortunately, she gave me an incorrect address, and the flowers I sent with a thank-you card and repayment were returned to me. Despite being unable to thank this earth angel properly, I will be forever grateful for her kindness. I'm sure that, as a student, she did not have a lot of money to spare. I'm also sure that life has repaid her kindness with multiple blessings.

- Plan exactly how you are going to get to your hotel from the airport. It is much safer when in a strange city to know how to get from the airport to your destination and the approximate cost and time before you leave.

- If you take a taxi from the airport, make it a point to notice the driver's identification. Also, call someone on your cell phone and let them know that you just got into a taxi on your way to the hotel. This way the driver knows that someone is expecting you at your destination.

- When booking a hotel, make sure that you research the area where it is located in order to ensure that you will feel safe. No matter how nice or expensive a hotel may be if it is located in a dangerous neighborhood your chances of falling victim to a crime increase.

- When checking in to the hotel, do not repeat your room number aloud or in earshot of others while at the front desk or anywhere in the lobby. If you see a suspicious character, situation, or just don't feel safe, ask the front desk to have someone escort you to your room.

- When you locate your room, gather your bearings. Know where the emergency exits and elevators are located. The layout of some hotel floors can be confusing, and you will not want to have to figure out the floor plan during an emergency.

- If the room assigned to you is located right next to an exit or has an adjoining room, ask to be moved. Unfortunately, you just never know who may be lurking in the stairwell or the intentions of your neighbor. The safest rooms in a hotel are usually located near heavy-traffic areas, the front desk, or main lobby. The key is to get a feel for the location of your room. If for whatever reason you do not feel safe with the location of your room, go back to the front desk and get another room, if possible.

- Once inside, keep the door lock bolted and the chain on at all times. In some cases, the bolt can be opened from the outside by the hotel staff, but the chain only operates from the inside. This will ensure that no one enters your room without your permission or awareness.

- If on a short trip, one to three days, you may want to consider keeping the 'do not disturb' sign on your door. This will mean that your room will not get cleaned, or the bed will be made, but it will increase your chances of keeping your belongings safe as no one should be violating your wishes for privacy.

- If you have not ordered room service or anything else from the concierge, do not open the door to anyone claiming they have a delivery for you. Use the peep-hole to identify the person that wants to get in and then call the front desk to verify.

- Watch what you eat. It is extremely easy to put on the pounds while traveling on business. Many of us tend to overeat when traveling and eat things we would normally not eat or drink at home.

- Many of us tend to view airplane food—if you get any—as a mere snack to hold us over until we can try some of the local cuisine. The increased calories and preservatives in airplane food make for an unhealthy meal.

- If your job requires extensive travel, try not to eat like you're on vacation. Also, try to remember that you do not have to be a member of the clean-plate club. Try to drink lots of water, and eat more of the light, healthy choices on the menu.

- Keep alcohol consumption in moderation. Because of the socializing during business events, some people tend to drink more when they are travelling. Alcohol can act as an appetite enhancer, and you will tend to eat more food if served with alcohol. Alcohol is usually high in empty calories, which provides little to no nutritional value to the body. These calories are in the form of simple carbohydrates and sugar, which can lead to weight gain. So not only do you increase your caloric intake via alcoholic beverages, but you also increase your appetite, a sure way to gain weight.

Traveling can be stressful, but if you plan ahead, you can make it a safe, pleasant and even relaxing experience. Sometimes traveling on an airplane or being alone in a hotel room is the only downtime I've had. I catch up on work, my personal reading, or movies.

Whether you are traveling for business or pleasure, the experience will be unique to you and your preferences. As you get more experienced in traveling, you will become well-versed in airline policies, airport security, hotel amenities, and enjoying time on the road.

The key is to minimize the stress and stay safe by planning ahead.

CHAPTER 11

DEVELOPING THE ROAD MAP
OF YOUR CAREER

Before you embark on the journey of your career, it is imperative that you develop a road map and a forward-looking perspective on your career. Just as you would not embark on a road trip without mapping out the route, you should not embark on your career journey without a road map. You should not just wander along; make a plan and take control of your career.

Take charge of your career by developing a road map that puts you in the driver's seat. Having clear direction regarding your career goals and aspirations will minimize your chances of ending up haphazardly moving along a path that does not bring the career satisfaction, reward, and achievement that you anticipated.

No matter what your career aspirations, it will serve you well to develop a road map, a personal marketing plan to help you along the way. If you are new to your organization or job, settle in and concentrate on mastering your current assignment. However, do not wait too long before you start planning your amazing career, which can be long and fruitful if you plan ahead.

A career road map will help you identify the best route to take to achieve your goals and help you stay on track. An effective career road map will enable you to determine the necessary steps required to develop your skills and expertise. It will help you maximize the opportunities that you will encounter along the way. It will allow you to develop strategies that will increase your career satisfaction and success.

Develop a three—or five-year plan. An effective plan should include detailed action steps and target completion dates. As you reach each milestone, celebrate your success, take a moment to rest, and then update your plan for the next three years. When updating your plan, include all of the new things that you have discovered along the way. Also, take a moment to look back and reassess the road you have just traveled, as it will help you map the route that will lead you to the next plateau.

Review your plan every year or so, to see if it requires tweaking or alternate route. There may be some circumstances that you had not anticipated that may require a change in direction. In other words, make this a living document and be flexible and open to potential changes.

In addition to having this career GPS (global positioning system), your plan will help you manage your time and resources. Few people take the time to develop a formal plan, having a plan will distinguish you from your peers and competition.

Below I have outlined some of the things that you may want to consider when developing and planning your career. This is not meant to be all-inclusive, and one size certainly does not fit all. So take what works for you, and leave the rest behind.

- **Your personal mission and vision.** Develop a personal career mission and vision statement. Your purpose statement goes beyond your job and defining goals. It includes everything in your career. It is your definition of success. It includes short—and long-term goals for where you want to be in the future.

  Your purpose can also encompass your passion, your life's mission, your reason for being. Identifying your purpose takes time and commitment. Try to develop a plan around your innate strengths and abilities, and in the process you will discover your true passion.

- **Develop a brand.** What is going to be your professional brand? What do you want your legacy to be? Self-branding is no different from the branding and marketing of a product. In order for a product to sell and be successful in the market, it has to have a good reputation and brand recognition. Self-branding is about discovering and figuring out what you want to do for the rest of your life; setting goals; writing down a career mission, vision and personal brand statement; and creating a development plan that is aligned with your personal purpose statement. Developing a brand and a marketing strategy will help you discover your abilities, strengths, and that distinctive element that makes you unique and marketable.

- **Ground Zero.** Identify your starting point. You must be brutally honest with yourself with respect to your current situation, where and how far you want to go or believe you can go, and how, who, or what can help you get to where you want to go. When identifying your ground zero, it is imperative that you fully understand and recognize your management's assessment of your potential and career path so you can realistically determine the amount of time it will take to reach your goals. Consider this a mission, and as with any mission, you need to state exactly what it is you want to accomplish and how you are going to accomplish it.

- **Goals.** Set long and short term goals. Short-term goals can be 90, 120, or 365 days. Your long-term goals should be where you see yourself within your company or industry in the next three to five years and how you are going to get there. These goals should be as specific and measurable as you can make them. They should be directly aligned with your career-development plans in conjunction with those your management envisions for you.

- **Action items.** Identify any changes, improvements, or action items that may be required in order to achieve your career goals and how you plan to close those gaps. These should include any actions that capitalize on your strengths, skills, and experience. Record these actions in chronological order, and assign each action step a target completion date. Your plan should include actions that you will need to help you master your current assignment and help propel you to that next plateau. For example, do you need to work on your leadership skills? How are your oral and written communication skills? Are there any deficiencies you need to work on improving?

- **Target position.** Identify a position you would like to be considered for and prepare a marketing campaign for that product called *You.* Why are you the best person for this job? What do you bring to the table that will benefit the corporation? Do you possess a skill that may give you a competitive edge? Are you bilingual, do you have exceptional skills in technology, spreadsheets, or other valuable skill set that distinguishes you from the competition?

- **Roadblocks.** Anticipate any potential roadblocks and develop a strategy to help you overcome some of those barriers. For example, is your current supervisor supportive of your plans or is he perceived to be a roadblock? If your immediate supervisor is perceived to be a roadblock, then you need to identify and address the issue as soon as possible. No amount of hard work and determination will help you get ahead if you do not have supportive management that believes in you and your abilities.

- **Resources.** Identify the resources available to assist you in achieving your career plans. These resources might include, but are not limited to, key people with specific expertise, training courses, networking, your boss, Human Resources, colleagues, working on a high visibility project, or employee resource group within your company that can help you enhance your leadership skills and confidence.

- **Engage Mentors.** Get several mentors who can help you achieve and meet your plan. Strive for a balance of male and female mentors, because there will be times when you will need advice from both.

- **Network.** If you are serious about your career you need to learn how to network and let people know about you. Give your brand the visibility it requires to get a good reputation. Not only do you need to get to know people, but people need to get to know you. If you learn the art of leveraging your personal style, values, and talents, and mastering the art of self-promotion, you can attain the success you deserve.

As you develop your plan, remember that your career requires that you take a holistic approach. It requires that you be well rounded in your experiences and education always understanding and abiding by those unwritten rules and regulations of the corporate environment.

CHAPTER 12

ASSESSING THE JOURNEY OF YOUR CAREER

Your career is a journey, not a destination—a journey that is defined by your choices, actions, reactions, and inactions to the opportunities and challenges life presents to you.

On that journey, you will encounter many different conditions along the way. There will be times when there is no congestion, no accident, traffic is light, and everything falls into place. Other times you will be traveling along a rocky road with many bumps, potholes, twists, and turns. A road that seems to be never-ending as one incident after the other causes you stress. Along that journey, you may come up to a dead-end, feeling stuck in a rut that seems impossible to overcome or get caught up in a never-ending loop, where no matter what you do—right or wrong—you seem to go nowhere but back where you started.

Learn to trust your intuition and gut feelings, and let your inner compass guide you along the way. There will be no signs pointing out directions or written or unwritten rules to ensure your success. To achieve your greatest aspirations, you will have to exhibit the courage to take risks, and explore new territory, which may mean facing difficult situations that could potentially result in failure.

Failure is not an accident; it is the result of actions, inactions, and reactions to your environment or situation. So if you do encounter failure, stop blaming others for your limitations or failures and look to the one place where limitations and insecurities breed and can be transcended: *in your own mind.* Do not give power to failure and trust your inner compass to map out the route to a successful journey. In life, nothing happens by accident or coincidence, and every experience is merely a stepping stone on the road to that next stage in your career.

Along your journey, there will be challenges and tough times, but it is imperative that you choose to regard these as opportunities and not roadblocks. Even though you may not understand the why or the how, embrace the challenges you encounter and view them as learning opportunities. If nothing else, you can learn something from a difficult situation, something that you can use to help you at a later stage. More often than not, some of these challenges turn out to be blessings in disguise.

Deciding to learn something from a difficult situation is the best strategy for coping with adversity. By simply asking what you can learn from a bad situation, you have changed your mindset. By changing your attitude, you stop focusing on being the victim and instead take control by choosing to make the adverse situation part of your informal education. The stumbling block becomes the stepping stone that will position you for that next career opportunity.

It will be extremely difficult for you to move forward with your career goals as long as you are fixated on a victim mentality. Unfortunate events are a fact of life and need to be separated from your personal self-worth. It's not what happens to you, but how you react to what happens to you that sets your life in motion. As you grow and mature in your career, you will make good decisions that will propel you to new heights. At times you will make poor decisions that may cost you a career move. Your response to life's unfortunate events will determine how smooth or rocky your journey will be, and how many of those plateaus you can reach.

Wholeheartedly master your current assignment, so that experience can lead you to the next plateau of your career. Every goal, milestone, or change is accomplished one action at a time. So continue along your path toward the realization of your goals, remembering that every road is traveled one step at a time.

Your career will be assessed by your integrity, the choices you made along the roads you travelled, the people you inspired to reach their full potential, and the lessons you learned. It will be defined by your actions, reactions, and inactions in light of the opportunities and challenges life presented to you.

Defining your career is not necessarily all about the company you work for, your job title, your salary or other perks. It is really about your self-evaluation, your sense of accomplishment, and your ability to define success for yourself, rather than letting others define it for you.

When planning the journey of your career, don't settle for a good or even great career; make *exceptional* your benchmark.

The choice is yours. You decide.

References

The "Vision Thing"—Critical to Accelerating Women's Careers, By Suzanne Bates; Career Promotion Work Bloom; February 27, 2009

"Why there are Differences in Gender Behavior" http://ebiz.netopia.com/learntolead/whyaretheredifferencesingenderbehavior/

Getting Beyond Career Failure; By: Victoria L. Rayner; Posted: June 26, 2008, from the July 2008 issue of Skin Inc. Magazine; http://www.skininc.com/spabusiness/management/personnel/21804394.html

"Mothers hone leadership skills on career breaks", By Robin Gerber; USAToday.com, January 8, 2003

Angelou, Maya. *Goodreads.com*. Web. <http://www.goodreads.com/author/quotes/3503.Maya_Angelou>.

Albert, Camus. ""Life Is a Sum of All Your Choices."—Albert Camus | Quotes | Dictionary of Quotes." *Quotes : Dictionary of Quotes*. Web. 15 Aug. 2011. <http://www.dictionary-quotes.com/life-is-a-sum-of-all-your-choices-albert-camus/>.

Burg, Bob. *Finestquotes.com*. Web. <http://www.finestquotes. com/author_quotes-author-Bob%20Burg-page-0.htm>.

Churchill, Winston. *Presentoutlook.com*. Web. <http:// presentoutlook.com/success-is/>.

Cloud, Glenda. *Quoteworld.org*. Web. <http://quoteworld. org/quotes/2940>.

Confucius. *Brainyquote.comj*. Web. <http://www.brainyquote. com/quotes/quotes/c/confucius101164.html>.

Drucker, Peter. *Finestquotes.com*. Web. <http://www. finestquotes.com/author_quotes-author-Peter%20Drucker- page-0.htm>.

Edison, Thomas A. *Buzzle.com*. Web. <http://www.buzzle. com/articles/short-inspirational-quotes.html>.

Fahmy, Miral. Reuters.com. Web. <http://www. reuters.com/article/2008/08/20/us-women-careers- idINSP29843720080820>. Reuters printed the findings in an article entitled "Career women are their own worst enemies: study".

Freud, Sigmund. *Goodreads.com*. Web. <http://www. goodreads.com/quotes/show/94440>.

Goldsmith, Oliver. *Brainyquote.com*. Web. <http://www. brainyquote.com/quotes/quotes/o/olivergold121314.html>.

Green, Dennis. *Dictionary Quotes*. Web. <http://www. dictionary-quotes.com/the-secret-to-success-is-to-start-from- scratch-and-keep-on-scratching-dennis-green/>.

Larsen, Christian D. *Beliefnet.com*. Web. <http://www. beliefnet.com/Quotes/Inspiration/C/Christian-Larson/ Believe-in-yourself.aspx>.

Luther King, Martin. *Empoweredquotes.com*. Web. <http:// empoweredquotes.com/2009/03/13/martin-luther-king-streetsweeper/>.

Olatunji, Babatunde. *Brainyquote.com*. Web. <http://www. brainyquote.com/quotes/authors/b/babatunde_olatunji. html>.

Rohn, Jim. *Personaldevelopmenttraining.com*. Web. <http:// www.personal-development-training.com/2010/02/jim-rohn-quotes.html>.

Roosevelt, Eleanor. *Quotationbooks.com*. Web. <http:// quotationsbook.com/quote/20848/>.

Roosevelt, Eleanor. *Self-improvementmentor.com*. Web. <http:// www.self-improvement-mentor.com/famous-leadership-quotes.html>.

ABOUT THE AUTHOR

Blanca's family emigrated from the Dominican Republic to New York City in 1963. During this time, the Hispanic population in New York City was small with no Latino Community to help with assimilation and ascension within the dominant English-speaking culture. With no one to help ease the difficulties of transition, there were plenty of opportunities to stumble linguistically and culturally. Given the Public School curriculum was English only and English was not offered as a second language, total immersion was the only option. She grew up on the upper west side of Manhattan in New York City's Public Housing (Projects), attended Mabel Dean Bacon (NYC Public High School), and graduated from Pace University with a Bachelor's Degree in International Business Management in 1985.

Blanca started her corporate career in 1982. In her 34 years with Mobil/ExxonMobil Corporation, she held numerous positions both domestic and international in nature with increasing responsibility. These assignments took her around the United States, Europe, Central / South America, and Nigeria.

She served as President/Vice President (2007 – 2010) of ExxonMobil's Employee Resource Group, a group designed to facilitate and promote the business, professional growth, and advancement of Hispanics throughout the company. As President, she often represented her company at numerous university and high school campuses promoting the company's commitment to higher education within the math and science fields.

She often represented her company as lead presenter at the Regional and National Scholarship Awards hosted by the Hispanic Heritage Foundation. In addition, she represented her company as host, keynote speaker, and panelist of various events with organizations supported by ExxonMobil's Foundation.

After thirty-four years in the industry, her most rewarding role was serving as mentor to the young employees in her company—guiding them through the corporate maze.

CPSIA information can be obtained
at www.ICGtesting.com
Printed in the USA
FFHW020937201218
49943580-54593FF